CENTRE FOR EDUCATIONAL RESEARCH AND INNOVATION

INDICATORS OF EDUCATION SYSTEMS

W9-CWE-738

EDUCATION POLICY ANALYSIS

1997

ORGANISATION FOR ECONOMIC CO-OPERATION AND DEVELOPMENT

ORGANISATION FOR ECONOMIC CO-OPERATION AND DEVELOPMENT

Pursuant to Article 1 of the Convention signed in Paris on 14th December 1960, and which came into force on 30th September 1961, the Organisation for Economic Co-operation and Development (OECD) shall promote policies designed:

- to achieve the highest sustainable economic growth and employment and a rising standard of living in Member countries, while maintaining financial stability, and thus to contribute to the development of the world economy;
- to contribute to sound economic expansion in Member as well as non-member countries in the process of economic development; and
- to contribute to the expansion of world trade on a multilateral, non-discriminatory basis in accordance with international obligations.

The original Member countries of the OECD are Austria, Belgium, Canada, Denmark, France, Germany, Greece, Iceland, Ireland, Italy, Luxembourg, the Netherlands, Norway, Portugal, Spain, Sweden, Switzerland, Turkey, the United Kingdom and the United States. The following countries became Members subsequently through accession at the dates indicated hereafter: Japan (28th April 1964), Finland (28th January 1969), Australia (7th June 1971), New Zealand (29th May 1973), Mexico (18th May 1994), the Czech Republic (21st December 1995), Hungary (7th May 1996), Poland (22nd November 1996) and the Republic of Korea (12th December 1996). The Commission of the European Communities takes part in the work of the OECD (Article 13 of the OECD Convention).

The Centre for Educational Research and Innovation was created in June 1968 by the Council of the Organisation for Economic Co-operation and Development and all Member countries of the OECD are participants.

The main objectives of the Centre are as follows:

- *to promote and support the development of research activities in education and undertake such research activities where appropriate;*
- *to promote and support pilot experiments with a view to introducing and testing innovations in the educational system;*
- *to promote the development of co-operation between Member countries in the field of educational research and innovation.*

The Centre functions within the Organisation for Economic Co-operation and Development in accordance with the decisions of the Council of the Organisation, under the authority of the Secretary-General. It is supervised by a Governing Board composed of one national expert in its field of competence from each of the countries participating in its programme of work.

Publié en français sous le titre :
ANALYSE DES POLITIQUES ÉDUCATIVES 1997

TABLE OF CONTENTS

Chapter 5

RESPONDING TO NEW DEMAND IN TERTIARY EDUCATION

INTRODUCTION
Making Educational Investment Effective

The 1990s have seen a growing recognition of the need for everyone in OECD countries to engage in lifelong learning, in order to participate fully in societies and economies that have come to revolve around the production and use of knowledge. But the measurement of knowledge and skills and of their benefits, is still imperfect. Only with an improved understanding of the value yielded by competencies during different phases in the lifespan will it be possible to make informed decisions about effective human capital investment.

Education has many benefits, some of them unquantifiable. Social cohesion rather than narrow economic gain is the greatest prize for societies in which all citizens through learning become more effective participants in democratic, civil and economic processes. No equation can fully describe this relationship. But education indicators can help us understand some of the contributing factors. How much do various forms of education contribute to people's employment prospects, to the literacy skills they need in everyday life, or to their prospective earnings? What are the spill-over effects of higher levels of education on the economic and social well-being of society as a whole?

Higher levels of educational attainment are clearly associated, for individuals, with higher earnings, lower chances of unemployment, and more skills that yield advantages to people as consumers and active citizens. The return on educational investment for whole societies is substantial, but more elusive. If certificates of educational attainment serve partly to "filter" rewards to relatively high achievers, rising educational attainment will not in itself create more rewards for society as a whole. It is certainly possible and desirable that a rise in the general level of relevant skills creates across-the-board gains, since too many adults lack some of the basic competencies needed to function well in knowledge-oriented societies. But for more education to serve this purpose, it needs to be well-designed. The educational performance of nations, and their efforts to improve it, cannot simply be based on the quantity of initial schooling, but derives from a range of other desirable characteristics.

First, the value of learning beyond initial schooling and tertiary education needs to be given due weight. Policies aiming to enhance the competencies of the population within a reasonable time-span must do as much to encourage adult learning as to improve the education of young people coming of age. This requires an understanding of what kind of adult programmes are effective – in particular, in enhancing general skills that equip people to respond flexibly to the challenges of twenty-first century life.

Second, the expansion of tertiary education cannot be divorced from the issue of the character and aptness of these studies. When post-compulsory education was a privilege of the elite, the advantage that it yielded for individuals was clear-cut: their employability and earnings were greatly enhanced, partly because diplomas, being scarce, made them distinctive. With mass participation, that advantage may be reduced for some graduates, particularly when there are large quality differences between institutions. Graduate unemployment has become a significant issue in some countries. Governments and individuals are looking more carefully at which courses have the best outcomes. Tertiary education is becoming increasingly heterogeneous. Matching the ongoing learning needs of all people beyond secondary school with individual course characteristics and prospects requires flexibility. These needs will not always be best met in university institutions, and not always immediately after leaving secondary education.

Third, the content of education at all levels must relate to the skills that students will need in adult life. The International Adult Literacy Survey has shown that a significant number of people with high academic credentials are unable to perform reading and mathematics tasks at a high level in everyday situations. Initial education thus needs to become better at developing the skills students require. The survey results have a profound relevance for the curricula of primary and secondary education, as well as for adult basic education.

In other words, investment in education cannot be measured merely along the single dimension of level of initial scholastic attainment, for it involves many different aspects of learning in a lifetime context. If each course of study becomes part of a specific learning pathway unique to an individual, then it will become even more difficult to predict the "return" that will result from obtaining a qualification at any particular level. Direct assessments of skill might offer a way of improving information and hence reducing the risk of market failure. Might unpredictability discourage private or public investment in education and training? Not if there is also an awareness of the *cost* of allowing a section of the population to be excluded from a learning-oriented society.

A world in which information flows plentifully and freely creates opportunities for wider social and economic participation, but also the danger of a new polarisation between those more and less able to access these opportunities. The International Adult Literacy Survey has shown that a significant proportion of the population in the countries surveyed could improve their life chances by improving their skill level. Everywhere at least a quarter of the population – and in some countries as many as a half – do not perform at the level considered by experts as a minimum for coping with the complex demands of modern life and work; they are therefore likely to be limited by relatively low literacy skills in some aspects of their job and life chances. In about a half of the OECD Member countries, 25 per cent or more of young people do not complete upper secondary education. Ministers of education have agreed that a full cycle of secondary education is needed as a foundation for all young people; without it they face severe risks on the labour market. Creating a society in which everyone can participate fully still requires raising the basic level to which all are educated.

To avoid a new polarisation, governments need to focus on the conditions of those who appear to face recurring difficulties from early childhood through adulthood. Failure to engage constructively in learning at school can create a core of adults who are distanced from full social and economic participation. Timely intervention to develop positive attitudes to learning is an investment that can bring high social returns. It is not simply a question of trying to encourage a higher proportion of young people to undergo more years of education. Expanded participation in tertiary education has not so far undone the great inequalities in rates of participation among social groups, since most of the places continue to be taken up by people from relatively privileged backgrounds. Other problems are that, in many countries, survival rates in tertiary education are not as high as they should be, and that many young adults encounter difficulties on the labour market even after graduating.

Policies to increase equity and efficiency in education and training should therefore consider carefully not only the incentives for pursuing further studies, but also the quality of and attitudes to learning in a lifetime perspective. They should aim to ensure that as many young adults as possible gain positive and constructive experiences of learning, on which they can continue to build throughout adulthood. Human capital investment, like investment in physical assets, needs to be constantly renewed. One of the most telling indicators in the years ahead will be the rate at which adults engage in organised education or training and self-directed learning. So far, such learning activities have been heavily concentrated among those with the greatest amount of initial schooling. If that distortion were reduced, a "learning society" would be closer to reality.

This report is published on the responsibility of the Secretary-General of the OECD.

Data sources and methods

The numeric values used for the production of the figures presented in the text are given in the corresponding tables in the Statistical Annex.

Additional statistical information, explanations, and technical notes describing calculation methods, data sources and issues concerning the reliability and comparability of the statistics presented here can be found in Annex 3 of the companion volume, *Education at a Glance: OECD Indicators.*

CHAPTER 1
EXPENDITURES ON EDUCATION

SUMMARY

Governments currently place a high priority on both maintaining the quality of their education systems, and containing overall public spending. Thus, they want to be sure that sufficient resources are devoted to education, and also that money is being well spent. On both counts, international comparisons can provide useful reference points, though not definitive answers.

The overall share of national income devoted to education is not closely linked to the income level of each country, even though richer countries tend to spend relatively more on each student. A key influence on total spending is the number of students enrolled. This is affected by the size of the youth population: in some countries, the effect of small youth cohorts can mean that 15-20 per cent less total spending is potentially needed than in the average OECD country. Another factor, more amenable to policy influence, is the proportion of young people enrolled in education, before and after the compulsory schooling age. Those countries with the smallest youth cohorts tend to have higher than average participation rates, with the cost to some extent balanced by the saving from the low youth population. In many countries there has been a trend towards higher participation as the size of the youth population falls.

Within compulsory schooling, the structure of resources devoted to each pupil varies widely between countries. Not only do teachers' salaries differ greatly, but the amount of teacher time devoted to each student per year can be twice as high in some countries than in others. This indicator is determined by the ratio of pupils to teachers, and the number of hours that each teacher must spend in the classroom in the course of a year. Together with teacher salaries, it determines the cost of delivering a given amount of instruction per student.

Various groups of countries can be distinguished, including some that put more into salaries but contain costs through high teaching loads, some that make lower demands on teachers but pay them less, and others in which both teaching requirements and salaries push costs in the same direction. By assessing separately the effects of each factor, it is possible to calculate the cost implications of having a structural feature that varies from the OECD average. For example, in several countries that require each teacher to spend relatively few hours in the classroom, the resulting salary costs are over 20 per cent higher than they would be if teaching hours were average for the OECD, while student instruction time and teacher salaries were kept the same.

In reality, policy-makers are severely constrained in the way they allocate resources, by the structures and traditions of their country's education system, by collective bargaining mechanisms and by other policy objectives not related to spending considerations. However, an awareness of spending patterns in other OECD countries, and of how much more or less it costs to differ from an international average, can contribute to the knowledge base that influences educational decision-making.

1.1 INTRODUCTION

In almost all OECD countries, total education expenditure accounts for between 5 and 8 per cent of GDP. The public portion of this represents between 10 and 15 per cent of public spending. This is a substantial proportion of national income by any standard. Under current conditions of tight public budget constraints, such a large spending item is subject to close scrutiny by governments looking for ways to trim or limit the growth of expenditure, often in the face of significant opposition by important stakeholders such as parents, teachers and employers.

In reappraising the amount spent on education, governments need to take a view both on how much education should be provided and on how well existing resources are being used. International comparisons cannot give direct answers to these questions, but knowledge about how different countries allocate resources can put each country's spending decisions in a wider perspective. This chapter looks at what lies behind differences in educational expenditures across OECD countries, and at some of the consequences of these variations for teaching and learning processes.

Is enough being spent on education? Each country's answer will depend, among other things, on how much education it is deemed appropriate to provide to young people, given current social norms and labour market requirements. While there is no universal answer, international comparisons can provide points of reference in terms of decisions taken by countries at comparable levels of economic development. Appropriate spending levels will also depend on how much it costs to provide education of a particular type. The relationship between resources and inputs (for example, teaching hours)differs considerably across countries, according to the organisation of instruction, the salaries of teachers, the type of instruction, and a host of other factors. The data analysis presented below goes some way in describing these differences, although it does not take account of the quality of inputs, notably teacher quality.

Is education spending effective? The question of whether the large sums devoted to education

are yielding value for money, in terms of student outcomes, figures prominently on the public agenda. There is some evidence within countries that money can matter to results (see Box 1A, page 21). However, current evidence shows no straightforward relationship across countries between spending levels and outcomes. In recent assessments of students in mathematics and science, for example, students in some OECD countries with relatively low per student expenditure have been among the best performers (OECD, 1996). This chapter restricts its analysis to differences in the ways in which educational resources are deployed, rather than on their final effectiveness.

1.2 EDUCATION SPENDING AND NATIONAL INCOME

There is considerable variation in the percentage of GDP devoted to education in different OECD countries. At the extremes, Greece and Turkey spend below 3.5 per cent; Denmark and Canada above 7 per cent (see data for Figure 1.1 in the Statistical Annex, page 98, right-hand column). But most countries fall within a much narrower band, half of them spending between 5 and 6 per cent of GDP. Moreover, if the two lowest spenders are excluded, there is no discernible relationship between how "rich" a country is in terms of national income per head and the proportion of this income that it allocates to education.

However, the amount that a country spends per student does tend to be higher for richer and lower for poorer countries. It is not surprising that more dollars are spent per student in countries where GDP per capita is high, since teacher salaries, the biggest component of educational expenditure, tend to be higher in these countries. But even if one controls for national income levels, by expressing expenditure per student as a percentage of GDP per capita, a relationship is found. As illustrated in Figure 1.1, countries with higher national income per head tend to spend proportionately more of this income on each student. In 11 of the 16 countries with per capita GDP above 16 000 dollars, the cost of educating one student is above 25 per cent average national income per person; whereas in the nine countries where GDP is below 16 000 dollars per head,

Figure 1.1
National income and spending per student
GDP per capita and expenditures on educational institutions per student as a percentage of GDP per capita, 1994

Dépenses par élève en pourcentage du PIB

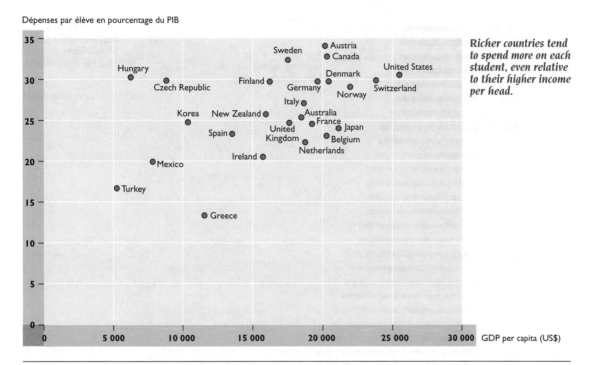

Richer countries tend to spend more on each student, even relative to their higher income per head.

Source: OECD Education Database.
Data for Figure 1.1: page 98.

the cost exceeds 25 per cent only in three, including the Czech Republic and Hungary, where education spending is high for historical reasons.

A variety of factors influence spending per student, some of them discussed in Sections 1.4 and 1.5 below. But first it is important to consider the other determinant of the overall education bill for each country: the total number of students.

1.3 EDUCATION SPENDING AND ENROLMENT

The most obvious factor influencing overall spending on education is the number of students enrolled. Since the majority of students are young people engaged in an initial period of education, overall enrolment levels are determined mainly by size of the youth population and by the proportion of each age-group being educated.

In OECD countries, the proportion of the total population that is aged between 5 and 29 varies from less than 32 per cent in Germany, Sweden and Switzerland to over 50 per cent in Turkey and Mexico, with an average of a little under 37 per cent (see Figure 1.2, page 12). The larger the size of this population, the more a country will have to spend on education, without this necessarily having any implications for educational quality.

While countries have little control over the size of their youth populations, the proportion who participate at various levels of education is a central policy issue. Variations in enrolment rates across countries reflect differences in the demand for education, in the extent of compulsory schooling and in policies regarding enrolment in the non-compulsory sectors of the education system, which include pre-primary schooling as well as tertiary and adult education.

Figure 1.2
The relative youth population
Population aged 5-29 as a percentage of the total population, 1995

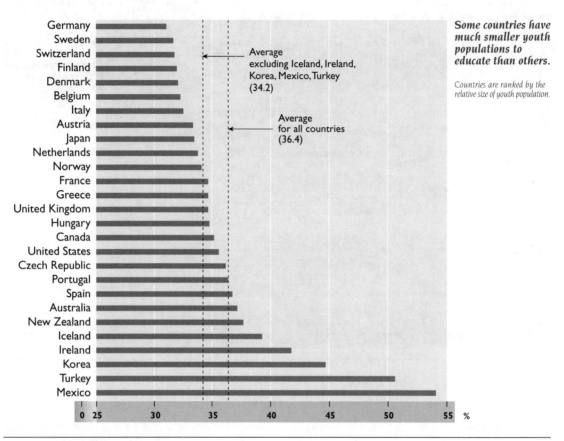

Average
excluding Iceland, Ireland,
Korea, Mexico, Turkey
(34.2)

Average
for all countries
(36.4)

Some countries have much smaller youth populations to educate than others.

Countries are ranked by the relative size of youth population.

Source: OECD Education Database.
Data for Figure 1.2: page 98.

Figures 1.3a and 1.3b show the proportion of young people enrolled at four key ages, near the beginning and near the end of compulsory schooling. The considerable differences have a substantial impact on the measured amount of national income devoted to education. The proportion of 3- and 5-year-olds involved in some form of pre-school programme gives an indication of the resources devoted to early childhood education. In Belgium, France and New Zealand, over 80 per cent of 3-year-olds are already enrolled in some form of pre-school programme whereas in Korea, Finland and Turkey, less than half are enrolled at 5, an age at which education in some OECD countries is already compulsory.

By age 17, a significant number have already left secondary education in some countries; in Korea and Portugal compulsory education ends as early as 14 (see Chapter 4 for the final age at which schooling is compulsory). But completion of the upper secondary stage is fast becoming the norm in most countries, and in Belgium, Germany and the Netherlands education in some form, usually part-time, remains compulsory until 18. Indeed, even at the age of 20 the majority of the population is still enrolled – either in secondary or in tertiary education – in Belgium, Canada, France and the Netherlands. In the Czech Republic, Mexico and Turkey, on the other hand, less than 25 per cent of 20-year-olds are enrolled.

Figure 1.3
Youth participation in education
Around the start of compulsory schooling and earlier...

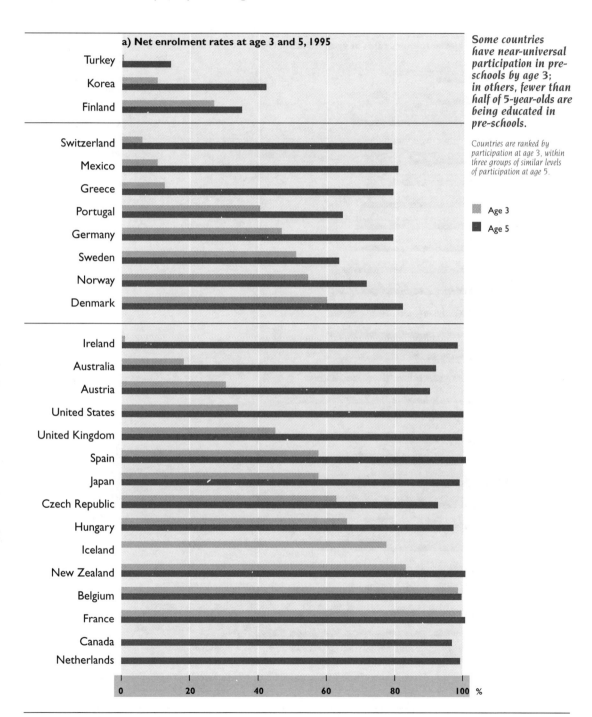

a) Net enrolment rates at age 3 and 5, 1995

Turkey
Korea
Finland

Switzerland
Mexico
Greece
Portugal
Germany
Sweden
Norway
Denmark

Ireland
Australia
Austria
United States
United Kingdom
Spain
Japan
Czech Republic
Hungary
Iceland
New Zealand
Belgium
France
Canada
Netherlands

0   20   40   60   80   100 %

Some countries have near-universal participation in pre-schools by age 3; in others, fewer than half of 5-year-olds are being educated in pre-schools.

Countries are ranked by participation at age 3, within three groups of similar levels of participation at age 5.

Age 3
Age 5

Source: OECD Education Database.
Data for Figure 1.3: page 98.

Figure 1.3 *continued*
Youth participation in education
Around the end of compulsory schooling and later…

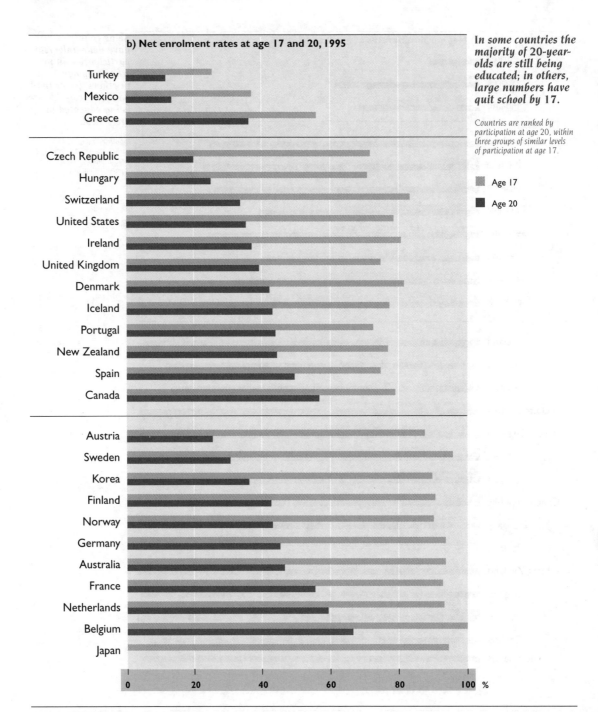

b) Net enrolment rates at age 17 and 20, 1995

In some countries the majority of 20-year-olds are still being educated; in others, large numbers have quit school by 17.

Countries are ranked by participation at age 20, within three groups of similar levels of participation at age 17.

Age 17
Age 20

Turkey
Mexico
Greece

Czech Republic
Hungary
Switzerland
United States
Ireland
United Kingdom
Denmark
Iceland
Portugal
New Zealand
Spain
Canada

Austria
Sweden
Korea
Finland
Norway
Germany
Australia
France
Netherlands
Belgium
Japan

0　　20　　40　　60　　80　　100 %

Source: OECD Education Database.
Data for Figure 1.3: page 98.

Figure 1.4
The effect of youth population and participation rate on spending
Contribution of the youth population and of enrolment rates to higher or lower education expenditures
as a percentage of GDP, relative to the OECD average, 1995

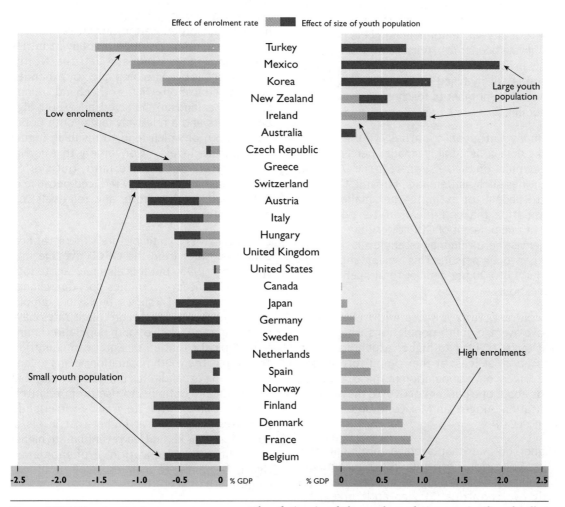

Source: OECD Education Database.
Data for Figure 1.4: page 99.

*The relative size of the youth population can significantly affect
education costs. Variations in the rate at which young people participate
in education can diminish or accentuate this effect. These factors can
raise or lower education spending by over 1 per cent of GDP.*

Countries are grouped to show common characteristics.

But exactly how much difference can variations in the size of the youth population or the rate of participation make to expenditure levels? Figure 1.4 shows the impact each of these factors has on each country's spending, compared to what spending would be if demography and participation (percentage of 5-29 year-olds enrolled)

were average for the OECD, and other things remained the same. For example in France, the fact that there are relatively few young people means that education spending can be 0.3 per cent of GDP lower than if the youth population were average and spending per young person in France were the same as it is now. But conversely, the fact that more of these young people are participating in education than elsewhere raises spending by 0.9 per cent of GDP above the level it would be if France had average participation rates. (However, it should be noted that these comparisons assume that spending per student does not vary with enrolment numbers. This has not always been true in practice over time, especially in cases where a falling school-age population is not matched by proportionate reductions in the number of teachers in compulsory schooling.)

In many European countries, young people make up a considerably smaller percentage of the population than elsewhere in the OECD. In countries such as Denmark, Finland, Germany and Sweden, for example, the smaller youth population makes educational expenditure about one per cent of GDP lower than it would otherwise be, assuming present levels of spending per young person. This "saving" represents about 15 to 20 per cent of total spending on education.

In contrast, Turkey, Korea and Ireland have above-average youth populations which in itself tends to lead to higher expenditures on education, at least at the compulsory stages. The larger youth population in these countries adds about one per cent of GDP to the national education budget. In Mexico, it adds two per cent of GDP.

Higher- or lower-than-average enrolment rates affect educational expenditures to a comparable magnitude, although in this case there are only two countries (Mexico and Turkey) for which the impact equals or exceeds 1 per cent of GDP. Figure 1.4 shows that in the cases where demography has the greatest potential impact on education costs compared to the OECD average, its impact is counterbalanced by participation rates with the opposite effect. It is true that demography and participation pull spending in the same direction in as many countries as they pull it in opposite directions. But in all four of the countries in which the effect of a small youth population is the greatest – potentially reducing spending by over 0.8 per cent of GDP – participation rates are above average; and in all three countries in which large youth

populations raise spending by over 0.8 per cent of GDP, participation is low.

This counterbalancing would seem logical. Countries with fewer young people can in principle afford to give more of them access to non-compulsory education, and vice versa. The fall in the youth population in many countries (Belgium, France, Germany and the Nordic countries) has been accompanied by expanded access to education. On the other hand, Ireland and New Zealand are characterised by both high enrolments and a relatively large youth population, both of which tend to result in higher expenditure levels. Conversely in Austria, Greece, Italy and Switzerland, outlays on education are significantly reduced because of both small youth cohorts and relatively low enrolments.

Figure 1.4 gives a static picture. It looks at how countries differ from the OECD average in a single year, 1995. But it is also relevant to look at how influences on countries' spending change over time. Figure 1.5 shows, by way of example, four countries in which enrolment rates have been rising and relative youth population falling – the typical situation in European countries. The drop in the youth population seems to lead to declining expenditures per GDP initially, but as enrolment continues to rise (from relatively low levels in Austria, Italy and Switzerland), increases tend to be at higher-cost levels of education. This should lead eventually to higher expenditures on education, a phenomenon that is beginning to manifest itself in all four countries.

Differences in relative spending levels across countries are therefore influenced not only by generous or frugal funding in relation to overall educational activity, but also by the level of this activity in terms of the number of students enrolled. Arguments to the effect that national spending levels are too low or too high compared to other countries therefore need to take account of structural features such as participation rates and the size of youth population. Given the magnitude of the effects described here, conclusions concerning the adequacy of the national effort devoted to education based on crude comparisons of spending as a percentage of GDP can be misleading.

Figure 1.5
Trends in demography, participation and spending
Changes in selected countries, 1975-1994

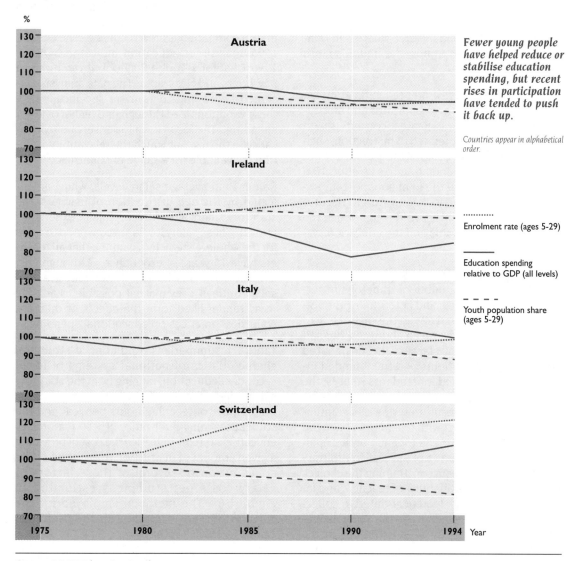

Fewer young people have helped reduce or stabilise education spending, but recent rises in participation have tended to push it back up.

Countries appear in alphabetical order.

....
Enrolment rate (ages 5-29)

———
Education spending relative to GDP (all levels)

– – – –
Youth population share (ages 5-29)

Source: OECD Education Database.
Data for Figure 1.5: page 99.

1.4 TEACHERS, STUDENTS AND THE ORGANISATION OF INSTRUCTION

The biggest component of educational expenditure is staff salaries, which in turn are dominated by the pay of teachers. So, an understanding of the determinants of teachers' pay is central to any explanation of how education spending varies.

On average, staff salaries account for about 82 per cent of current expenditures on education at the primary and secondary level in OECD countries, ranging from just under 65 per cent in the Czech Republic and Sweden to over 90 per cent in Greece, Italy, Portugal and Turkey (OECD, 1997). Around 10 per cent or less of staff salaries are accounted for by non-teaching staff in Austria,

Belgium, Ireland and Turkey, but close to 30 per cent in Denmark and the United States. It is interesting to note that in the first four of these countries, local government is the source of less than 5 per cent of public educational funds at the primary and secondary level, whereas in Denmark and the United States, the figure is close to 50 per cent.

Although the impact of non-teaching staff can be significant, both on expenditures and on educational processes, the greatest concern is with expenditures directly related to instruction, such as teacher salaries. Besides the significant impact which their remuneration has on education budgets, teachers are the final and most important link in the delivery of education to the students; they are the interface through which the objectives of the schools and the education system are mediated.

Education ministries and local decision makers need to consider a number of trade-offs in setting education budgets and determining the volume of educational activity. In the case of teaching, decisions must be taken about teacher salary level, the size of classes, the designated amount of teaching hours and the intended instruction time planned for students (that is, the length of the school year). The amount spent on education and the result in terms of the intensity of student contact with teachers will depend on what choices are made for each of these, although they are clearly not subject to arbitrary variation. The elements constraining the choices made include the availability of teachers and facilities, pay and work load negotiated in collective bargaining agreements and the absolute limits on expenditures imposed externally in the budgetary process. In addition the current structure of education systems and of schools represents a long history of decisions that reflect, as well as budgetary considerations, pedagogical choices concerning minimum teacher qualifications, class sizes and the amount of instruction deemed necessary to achieve specific curricular objectives.

International comparisons of total spending per student transmit imperfectly the costs and consequences of the decisions that have been made in these respects. But it is possible, by examining the various elements affecting spending per student, to quantify broadly how much certain national choices cost relative to the average for the countries investigated. This average is a somewhat artificial norm, but a necessary benchmark if comparisons are to be made. The OECD's 1996 analysis of education indicators (OECD, 1996, Chapter 4) took a first look at variations in pay, hours and class sizes. The data analysis presented below considers more specifically how these variations feed through into higher or lower spending. The focus is on lower secondary education – the level at which the relevant information is available for a range of countries.

Rather than average salary levels, which are affected by the age distribution of teachers, the statutory salary after fifteen years of experience is used. These salary levels are converted to costs for the whole system, by assuming that all teachers have 15 years of experience. Although cost estimates on this basis will not reflect actual salary outlays, they make it possible to analyse in a standardised form the effects of different countries' practices on educational spending.

Table 1.1 summarises a number of structural characteristics of national systems of lower secondary education, ranging from the statutory salary after 15 years of teaching experience, to the number of teaching hours per year and the student:teaching staff ratio. These features of education systems influence the cost of providing a given amount of instruction to each child. The contribution of several of these factors to salary costs per student is estimated in Figure 1.6. The methods employed for the calculations are explained in the Technical Annex to this chapter.

Table 1.1 calculates, in its final column, the average number of teacher hours devoted to each student. This brings together information on the total quantity of teaching time and on the number of students, and is a summary indicator of educational "input". One striking aspect is that even excluding Turkey, which is an outlier and therefore not shown in Table 1.1, the amount of teaching time devoted to each student over a year varies by a factor of more than two, from about 40 hours to almost 100 hours. In some cases, this variation can be accounted for almost

Table 1.1
Working conditions of teachers and instructional characteristics, lower secondary level, 1995

	Statutory salary after 15 years of experience (US Dollars)[1]	Instruction supplied per teacher in hours per year (teaching time)	Intended student instruction time in hours per year	Student: teaching staff ratio[2]	Statutory salary per teaching hour (US Dollars)[3]	Total (statutory) salary cost of teachers per student enrolled (US Dollars)[3]	Class size[3,4]	Teaching hours per student per year[3]
	A	B	C	D	E A/B	F A/D	G C*D/B	H B/D=C/G
Switzerland	50 400	1 056	–	12	48	4 098	–	86
Group 1								
Denmark	28 990	750	890	9	39	3 083	11	80
Belgium	28 360	720	987	7	39	3 832	10	97
Austria	26 200	651	1 084	9	40	2 922	15	73
Group 2								
Germany	37 060	712	950	16	52	2 342	21	45
Ireland	33 840	735	935	16	46	2 091	21	45
France	28 210	660	954	13	43	2 152	19	50
Group 3								
Italy	23 360	612	1 020	10	38	2 326	17	61
Norway	21 120	611	823	9	35	2 246	13	65
Group 4								
Netherlands	35 340	954	1 067	17	37	2 091	19	56
United States	30 460	964	980	18	32	1 706	18	54
Spain	28 020	900	900	16	31	1 702	16	55
Group 5								
Portugal	24 560	681	949	13	36	1 889	18	52
Sweden	20 310	576	828	12	35	1 658	18	47
Greece	16 420	569	927	13	29	1 235	22	43
Czech Republic	6 810	657	–	13	10	524	–	51
Korea	33 580	–	–	26	–	1 293	–	–
New Zealand	22 750	869	918	19	26	1 224	20	46
Average (all countries)	**27 544**	**746**	**947**	**14**	**36**	**2 134**	**17**	**59**
Average (excluding Korea)	**27 189**	**746**	**947**	**13**	**36**	**2 184**	**17**	**59**

– : missing value, or not applicable.
1. Adjusted using purchasing power parities.
2. Covers the entire secondary level for Belgium, France, Ireland and Portugal. Figure for Belgium is for 1994.
3. Derived values.
4. See Technical Annex, pages 26-27.
Source: OECD Education Database.

Countries are grouped according to their similarity on several characteristics. See text.

entirely by differences in the ratio of pupils to teaching staff – for example, Germany has more than twice as many pupils per teacher as Belgium, and consequently only just over half as much teaching time per student. But even in two countries with the same number of students for each teacher, pupils can receive on average widely different amounts of teacher attention, because of variations in the number of hours that each teacher must teach in a year. Greece and Switzerland have similar student:teaching staff ratios, but the far heavier teaching load in Switzerland results in pupils getting nearly twice as much total teacher time on average.

Countries in Table 1.1 have been grouped according to their similarity on several characteristics, and ordered by the average salary cost per student in each group. Switzerland, with high salary costs, and Korea and New Zealand with low ones, do not fit neatly into any group. Other countries have been divided into five groups, with roughly similar characteristics at lower secondary level:

- **Group 1:** *Teachers with small classes and few working hours make per-student costs high.* Austria, Belgium and Denmark have salary costs per pupil that exceed the OECD average by between one-third and one-half, even though teacher salaries are about average. The reason is that children in these countries spend long or average hours in small classes, yet each teacher has a lower than average work load. So a large number of teachers are needed, relative to the number of children.

- **Group 2:** *High salaries but large classes produce medium per-student costs.* Germany, France and Ireland show relatively high teacher salaries and large classes, which translates into mid-range values for both salary costs per student ($2 000 to $2 400) and teaching time per student (45 to 50 hours).

- **Group 3:** *Low salaries and low teaching hours result in medium per-student costs.* This group, consisting of Italy and Norway, shows both below average salaries (a little over $20 000) and particularly low teaching hours (near 610 hours). Together these combine to yield costs and instruction time per student that are above average. Because the teaching load is low relative to the length of the school year, this type of system ends up being somewhat expensive compared to the average.

- **Group 4:** *High teaching loads produce average to below average per-student costs despite above average salaries.* The Netherlands, Spain and the United States are characterised by only somewhat lower statutory salaries and class sizes, but average to below average salary costs per student ($1 700 to $2 100), largely as a result of higher teaching loads (some 900 to 950 hours per year). These countries illustrate the important distinction between student:teaching staff ratios and class size. A modestly-resourced system, in terms of teachers per enrolled student, can still have average size classes if teachers work long hours.

- **Group 5:** *Low salaries translate into low per-student costs, as short teaching hours are offset by classes that are average to above average in size.* Data for the fifth group, comprised of the Czech Republic, Greece, Portugal and Sweden are partial, but show relatively low salary costs per student, even though teaching hours are low for all the countries. The reason is that class sizes in these countries are large compared to Group 3, where salaries are also relatively low. Thus it takes fewer teachers to cover the same number of students as in Group 3. With the exception of the difference in salary levels, this group looks very much like Group 2.

What is striking is the heterogeneity observed across education systems. The complex arbitration in education budgeting between statutory salaries, the teaching load, the intended hours of instruction and the class size has been resolved in practice in a variety of ways. The rationale for the various choices made, however, is not obvious. If indeed the differences observed in the organisation of instruction reflect considered choices concerning the means to achieve system-wide educational objectives at the lower secondary level, there does not appear to be international consensus on these matters. Class sizes vary from about 11 students on average per class in Belgium and Denmark to about 21 students in Germany, Ireland and Greece. Teaching loads are about 570 hours per year in Greece and Sweden, but over 950 hours per year in the Netherlands and the United States and over 1 050 hours per year in Switzerland.

An obvious question of interest is whether these choices matter. As will be shown below, in budgetary terms they certainly do. Whether they also matter in relation to outcomes is a much more difficult question (see Box 1A). In particular, the data do not account for the effect of pedagogical decisions, which can be expected to influence the end result, but on which little

Box 1A   WHEN MONEY MATTERS

Does spending more on education make any difference to school achievement? About $1 trillion a year is now spent on education in OECD countries, yet fundamental problems such as widespread failure and under-achievement persist (see Chapter 4). Since James Coleman (1966) reported that resources make little difference to schools' performance once the characteristics of students were taken into account, policy-makers have been asking whether more money for education is necessarily a solution. Some argue that any attempt to reform education will fail without extra resources, to pay for more or better teachers, extra equipment and appropriate buildings that are needed to enhance all students' opportunity to learn. Others argue that it is more a matter of restructuring the way that existing resources are spent, making them more "productive" by concentrating on areas most likely to improve teaching and learning. Who is right?

Much of the evidence on how much of a difference extra spending makes to educational performance, collected over the past three decades, has been inconclusive or conflicting. Some studies have concluded that there is no systematic link between spending and student performance; others that there is a clear, if weak, positive relationship (see, for example, Hanushek, 1989; Hedges et al., 1994; and Lee et al., 1993). Some studies have employed highly aggregated data, making little distinction between different kinds of spending, and looking for simple and direct links between spending and achievement, rather than examining third factors, such as the learning environment of the school or time on task, which may be improved by certain kinds of spending and may in turn influence student performance. Furthermore, previous studies have not always accounted sufficiently for the effects of student background.

A recent study by the Educational Testing Service in the United States has overcome some of these problems by bringing together a rich mass of information on spending, school processes and student achievement from across the country (Wenglinsky, 1997). The United States makes an interesting laboratory because its 15 000 school districts spend greatly varying amounts on education within a broadly common system. This makes it possible to draw the kinds of comparisons that are not available from comparing countries (whose institutional frameworks differ), or from comparisons within countries or local government units that have broadly uniform spending patterns. Do U.S. school districts that spend more money get better results?

The answer is yes, in some respects. For both fourth and eighth graders, clear benefits in terms of student achievement were found as a result of increases in some aspects of spending on instruction. More spent on teachers, on other instructional resources and on district-level administrators all helped to lower the pupil:teacher ratio, which was found to contribute to student achievement. But whereas for fourth-graders (aged about 9) a low pupil:teacher ratio led directly to higher achievement, for eighth-graders (aged 13) the positive effect was mediated by an improved school environment.

These findings offer some support for those who believe that investing more in education will produce beneficial results. But they also lend credence to the view that this investment cannot be indiscriminate. The study found that although direct spending on teachers yielded identifiable results, spending on school-based administrators and on buildings did not. It also found that even though spending more on teachers helped raise their average qualifications, this had no discernible direct impact on student achievement. These specific results may well be particular to the institutional context of the United States. But for all countries, they indicate that spending can matter, although it is important to identify where it matters most.

comparative information is available. These might include, for example, the minimum teacher qualifications (which would influence the statutory salary and the quality of recruits), the curricular objectives (which might affect the hours of instruction per year), and the amount of homework or individualised instruction appropriate or necessary at the lower secondary level (a high level of which would be incompatible with a heavy teaching load).

1.5 HOW THE ORGANISATION OF INSTRUCTION AFFECTS COSTS

How, then, do the characteristics of the education systems described in Table 1.1 translate into higher or lower teaching costs per student? How much more does it cost an education system, for example, to have a teaching corps that works relatively few hours per year, as opposed to "average" teaching hours? Or by how much do higher statutory salary levels increase costs per student? Estimates of this kind, in which one feature of the education system is assumed to change while others remain fixed, need to be treated with caution because, as noted previously, they do not reflect the arbitration between the various features of the system that occurs in practice. Nonetheless, they are useful in placing an approximate cost figure on the particular features that characterise national education systems.

Figure 1.6 illustrates how various factors contribute to the statutory teacher salary cost per student in each country shown by the bars. The first category of estimates (Column A) shows the average of per-student salary cost for all OECD countries. Columns B to D show how much a particular factor influences this average, in terms of pulling it above or below the OECD average. Column B shows how much a country's per-student costs are compared with the situation if salaries in that country were average for the OECD and everything else was unchanged. The next two columns do the same for the number of teaching hours that each teacher must supply and the average teacher time devoted to each student. The more teacher hours are devoted to each

student at a given level of teacher salary and workload, the more teachers will be needed, so costs will be higher. Similarly, the longer the hours taught by each teacher, the lower will be the overall cost of supplying a given amount of instruction at a particular teacher salary.

In most countries, these three factors explain most of the difference between per-pupil salary costs in individual countries and the OECD average. But simultaneously changing two or more of the above factors can also have an influence, so the total variation of salary costs per pupil from the OECD average is slightly different from the sum of the influence of the three factors shown. This difference is shown as a residual factor in Column E.

The data for Germany, by way of example, show that the relatively high level of statutory salaries in that country adds US$624 per student to education costs compared to the average for the countries shown. On the other hand, because of larger class sizes, instruction time per student tends to be somewhat lower than average (see Table 1.1), and this makes it about $741 cheaper to cater for each student with a given amount of teaching time. But teachers in Germany have shorter than average teaching hours (712 per year compared with 746 on average for the OECD), so that it costs about $28 dollars per student more to provide a given amount of instruction. Adding together these three positive and negative effects gives a net sum of $89 to average OECD per-pupil salary costs ($2 184) to yield $2 095. In fact, the per-pupil salary cost in Germany is $2 342, so $247 of Germany's statutory salary costs per student are not accounted for by considering independently the effects of the three factors specified.

Figure 1.6 shows the degree to which countries in each of the five categories described above have higher or lower costs resulting from each aspect of the way they organise instruction. For example, for countries in Group 1 (Austria, Belgium and Denmark), high costs per student are most significantly influenced by giving children on average more teacher time in the course of a year, and to a smaller degree by having light teaching-hour requirements of

Figure 1.6

Teacher pay, teacher workload and teaching time per student: the cumulative effects on costs
Effects of various components on teachers' statutory salary costs[1] per student,[2]
relative to the country average, 1995

Country average statutory salary cost per student	Effects on student costs (Incremental or decremental effect of specified factor, in US Dollars per student, converted using purchasing power parities)				Country statutory salary cost per student enrolled	
	Level of statutory salary (after 15 years of experience)	Instruction supplied per teacher (hours)	Total teaching time per student (hours)	Residual		
A	B	C	D	E	A + B + C + D + E	
US$	US$	US$	US$	US$		
2 184	+1 887	-1 906	+1 271	+662	4 098	Switzerland
2 184	+158	+4	+1 500	-13	3 832	Belgium
2 184	+192	-125	+794	+39	3 083	Denmark
2 184	-110	+283	+538	+28	2 922	Austria
2 184	+624	+28	-741	+247	2 342	Germany
2 184	+78	+181	-379	+89	2 152	France
2 184	+411	-41	-636	+174	2 091	Ireland
2 184	-381	+351	+65	+107	2 326	Italy
2 184	-645	+342	+199	+167	2 246	Norway
2 184	+482	-677	-103	+205	2 091	Netherlands
2 184	+183	-576	-166	+80	1 706	United States
2 184	+50	-423	-141	+33	1 702	Spain
2 184	-202	+104	-247	+50	1 889	Portugal
2 184	-562	+333	-430	+133	1 658	Sweden
2 184	-810	+260	-474	+75	1 235	Greece
2 184	-1 569	+46	-90	-47	524	Czech Republic
2 184	-239	-252	-327	-143	1 224	New Zealand

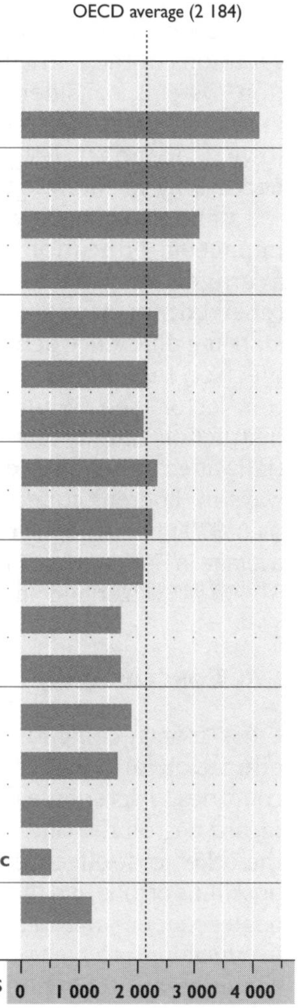

OECD average (2 184)

US$ 0   1 000   2 000   3 000   4 000

1. Teachers with 15 years of experience.
2. Lower secondary level.
Source: OECD Education Database.
Data for Figure 1.6: page 100.

If teachers are paid more, if each of them works less, or if students receive more total teacher attention, the cost of educating a student will be relatively high. This figure shows the cumulative effect on spending of variations from the OECD average of each component.

Countries are ranked as in Table 1.1 (see explanation in text).

staff. So if, for example, Austrian teachers were required to teach classes for 746 hours a year (the OECD average) rather than 651 as at present without changing salaries, class sizes or pupil instruction time, fewer teachers would be required and this would save $283 per student. But if Austria kept teaching hours the same and reduced the teacher time devoted to each student to the international average, the potential savings from employing fewer teachers would be nearly twice that amount – $538.

Figure 1.6 demonstrates that the national variations in the particular features of education systems considered here translate into major differences in spending priorities at the lower secondary level, in practice if not necessarily in intention. In many countries, the statutory salary level has a less significant impact on education costs relative to the average than the amount of instruction received per student. Perhaps the most startling difference across countries concerns precisely the relative amounts attributable to this factor (see Column D). The amount of instruction time received per student potentially affects spending levels in vastly different ways in different countries, reducing them by over $700 per student relative to the country average in Germany but increasing them by about $1 300 in Switzerland and $1 500 in Belgium.

1.6 CONCLUSIONS

Cross-country comparisons of expenditures on education provide useful benchmarks for countries to determine if national efforts in this regard are, on the one hand, adequate and on the other, cost-effective. With the continuous upskilling of jobs and the move towards a knowledge economy in OECD countries, investment in education is a high priority if economies and societies are to benefit from the effects of globalisation. But resources are not unlimited, and education, like other areas of spending, must compete for available resources.

Comparisons of expenditure levels by themselves can be misleading if seen out of context. "Richer" countries may tend to spend more on education, but returns may not be as high as in "poorer" countries or indeed as in the past, without additional efforts at improving the quality and efficiency of delivery. Expenditure levels across countries may vary by as much as a full percentage point of GDP because of differences in the relative size of the youth population and in enrolment rates. The intensity of national effort in regard to education or its cost-effectiveness cannot be assessed without taking such structural differences into account.

It is evident from the examination of the features of lower secondary systems presented in this chapter that there are a number of different "models" of how instruction at this level is to be organised and what elements of instruction (class sizes, annual instruction time, teaching load) are to be emphasised. With respect to the allocation of funds, the "models" are significantly different, although this is relative to an admittedly artificial norm.

The question of which model is better is a natural one, but not entirely appropriate. Each education system is a working system, which to a greater or lesser degree has satisfied the requirements of its society. The different "models" represent a long history of decisions taken nationally and are subject to a certain inertia that makes it difficult to introduce substantial changes over night, if for no other reason than that some features of the system are often subject to negotiation in the framework of collective bargaining agreements. The success of a model may depend on less quantifiable characteristics of the education system, such as the teaching methods used or the extent of remedial help available. The interplay between, for example, features such as class size and teaching methods is far from clear. Small classes may mean that more attention to individual students is possible, but in the absence of curriculum reform or of a change in teaching practices, for example, the expected benefits may not be forthcoming.

Although the choices made concerning the organisation of instruction do have major cost consequences, the relationship to student outcomes remains an unknown. An appropriate reform strategy would be based on identifying the determinants of learning effectiveness, which may well transcend the mechanics of how instruction is organised. But this should not prevent governments from taking due account of the important effect on educational spending of the diverse organisational routes chosen by various countries. When adapting their systems in the future, the fact that different models are shown to have very different spending implications will be an important consideration.■

References

COLEMAN, J.S. *et al.* (1966), *Equality of Educational Opportunity*, United States Government Printing Office, Washington, D.C.

HANUSHEK, E.A. (1989), "The impact of differential expenditures on school performance", *Educational Researcher*, Vol. 18(4), pp. 45-65.

HEDGES, L.V., LAINE, R.D. and GREENWALD, R. (1994), "Does money matter? A meta-analysis of studies of the effects of differential school inputs on student outcomes", *Educational Researcher*, Vol. 23(3), pp. 5-14.

LEE, V.E., BRYK, A.S. and SMITH, J.B. (1993), "The organisation of effective secondary schools", *Review of Research in Education*, Vol. 19, pp. 171-267.

OECD (1996), *Education at a Glance: Analysis*, Paris.

OECD (1997), *Education at a Glance: OECD Indicators*, Paris.

WENGLINSKY, H. (1997), *When Money Matters*, Educational Testing Service, Princeton, New Jersey.   ......

Technical Annex

Expenditures on education (denoted by X) as a percentage of GDP can be expressed as the product of a number of factors, as follows:

$$X/GDP = (X/S) * (S/Y) * (Y/P) * (P/GDP),$$

where S is the number of students 5 to 29 years of age, Y the population 5 to 29 years of age and P the total population. Expenditure per GDP is thus the product of expenditure per student, the enrolment rate, the youth population share and the reciprocal of GDP per capita.

The difference in expenditures per GDP between a particular country (referred to as country A) and any other country i can be broken down into the sum of the following terms:

$$
\begin{aligned}
(X/GDP)_A - (X/GDP)_i = \ & ((X/S)_A - (X/S)_i) * (S/Y)_A * (Y/P)_A * (P/GDP)_A \\
& + (X/S)_A * ((S/Y)_A - (S/Y)_i) * (Y/P)_A * (P/GDP)_A \\
& + (X/S)_A * (S/Y)_A * ((Y/P)_A - (Y/P)_i) * (P/GDP)_A \\
& + (X/S)_A * (S/Y)_A * (Y/P)_A * ((P/GDP)_A - (P/GDP)_i) \\
& + I
\end{aligned}
$$

where I is the so-called "interaction" and represents the sum of a number of terms involving the product of two or more of the factor differences. A typical term of this kind would be, for example:

$$((X/S)_A - (X/S)_i) * ((S/Y)_A - (S/Y)_i) * (Y/P)_A * (P/GDP)_A$$

The first term to the right of the equal sign can be interpreted as the portion of the difference in expenditures per GDP between the two countries attributable to the difference in expenditures per student, the second term as that attributable to the difference in enrolment rates, and so on.

If one then averages over all countries indexed by i, one obtains a formula similar to that given above except that the terms indexed by i are replaced by the country means for the given variables. The mean of the interaction terms, on the other hand, is not amenable to easy interpretation and is considered for the purposes of the analysis as a residual.

In Figure 1.4, the estimates of the effect of the size of the youth population and of enrolment rates on expenditures per GDP are given by the second and third terms of the formula above, but where the terms in i are replaced by the mean values.

Expenditures per student and full-time equivalent enrolment rates for all levels of education combined have been used and the age group 2-29 considered as a whole. However, both expenditures per student and enrolment rates vary by level of education and the size of individual age cohorts can also differ significantly. A more in-depth analysis might show contributions to expenditure levels different from those shown in this chapter (see, for example, indicator B1 in *Education at a Glance - OECD Indicators*, where some of these other factors have been accounted for in the calculations).

The measure of class size in Table 1.1 is calculated indirectly, by dividing the total number of hours spent in class by all students, by the total number of hours spent in class by all teaching staff. It is equivalent to a weighted average of class sizes, where each class is weighted by the number of hours it meets per year. This calculation assumes that reported teaching staff are involved exclusively in teaching, that only one teacher is present in a class at a given time and that there is no absenteeism of teaching staff. Deviations from these assumptions may result in estimates of average class size that may be different from those estimated directly from class size data.

The calculations for Figure 1.6 are comparable in nature. Statutory salary costs per student C can be expressed as the product of three factors, as follows:

$$C = W * T * / S = W * (t * T/S) * (1/t),$$

where W is the statutory salary after 15 years of experience, T is the number of full-time equivalent teachers, S is the number of full-time equivalent students and t is the annual teaching time. The term $t*(T/S)$ is what has been called in the text the annual instruction time received per student.

As in the previous case, the product above can be broken down as follows:

$$
\begin{aligned}
C_A - C_m = \ & (W_A - W_m) * (t * T/S)_A * (1/t)_A \\
& + W_A * ((t*T/S)_A - (t*T/S)_m) * (1/t)_A \\
& + W_A * (t * T/S)_A * ((1/t)_A - (1/t)_m) , \\
& + 1
\end{aligned}
$$

where the m subscript indicates the mean over all countries.

The four terms shown here are precisely the ones which figure in Figure 1.6. The first term can be interpreted as the portion of the difference between statutory salary costs per student in country A and average statutory salary costs that is attributable to the difference between the statutory salary in country A and the average statutory salary, the second term the portion attributable to the difference between the instruction time received per student in country A and the average value of this over all countries, and so on.

CHAPTER 2
LIFELONG INVESTMENT IN HUMAN CAPITAL

SUMMARY

Investment in education can have social and economic benefits, through the development of a greater bank of knowledge and skills, referred to as "human capital". There is strong evidence of the direct payoff of such investment to individuals, and a growing body of evidence that there are positive external effects for employers, communities and whole societies. But countries need to develop a better understanding of the relative effectiveness of investment in human capital formation in different institutions, and at different points in the lifespan. Investment cannot be restricted solely to an initial period of education and training, partly because this will change too gradually the skill profile of the whole workforce, and also because individuals need constantly to develop knowledge and competence to adapt to changing requirements.

Much of the focus so far has been on the knowledge and competence developed through initial schooling and tertiary education for young people. Attainment early in life is certainly important: those who complete upper secondary or tertiary education have greater chances of showing high levels of literacy proficiency, of being employed and of having higher earnings. Individual prospects now go up more at the margin as a result of participating in tertiary education than as a result of upper secondary schooling. This is especially true for women. For example, in countries where relatively few women are in the workforce, those with upper secondary education are not much more likely than average to be in employment in their thirties and forties, but those with an education at the tertiary level are as likely to work as similar women in other countries.

A full evaluation of the returns to education would take account not only of individual or private outcomes, but also of social benefits such as improved public health or reduced social disorder. But these are difficult to measure. Yet even looking at the return to public and private investment only in terms of earnings gains and resulting tax revenues, the estimated rate of return is in many cases above 10 per cent. It tends to be higher for upper secondary than for tertiary education, whose relatively large benefits are offset by much greater costs.

On present trends, there will be a gradual convergence of countries according to one measure of the human capital stock: the proportion of the adult population who have completed upper secondary schooling. This convergence could be considerably faster if the countries with the lowest-qualified work force continue to raise upper secondary completion rates for young people. Educational attainment could be increased even more quickly with an increase in the number of adults being educated.

However, educational attainment is only one aspect of human capital. Any investment strategy also needs to recognise the benefits of lifelong acquisition of knowledge and skills, for example through workplace learning. Participation in such activity has tended to be concentrated among those who already have high levels of initial education. Governments can play a role in encouraging job-related learning among a wide range of groups, but must do so in partnership with employers and individuals. Where resources are limited, it is important to look at cost-effective options such as part-time studies, distance learning and modular programmes that can address individual learning needs through a combination of learning while working, and working while learning.

2.1 INTRODUCTION

Education can be seen both as a good itself and as a means to social and economic ends. This chapter focuses on the latter, "instrumental" aspects of education, without trying to imply that these are more important than its intrinsic benefits. But the increasing emphasis on the role in economic growth of people's knowledge and skills, or "human capital", has helped make education and training more central to the concerns of governments. This interest arises not just for the sake of prosperity, but also for social well-being. Poor distribution of human capital can contribute to unemployment, social inequality and the disaffection of those excluded from full participation in the knowledge society.

Despite the recognition of the value of human capital development, national accounts still treat education mainly as consumption rather than investment. In fact it is both. But it is difficult to measure accurately the return on human capital investment, and correspondingly difficult to ensure that resources are deployed effectively to produce desired outcomes. This chapter looks at various options for policy-makers to enhance human capital. In analysing the prospective benefits of education and training at different levels, it argues that, to be effective, the investment needs to be balanced between the initial schooling and further education of young people and other measures to promote learning throughout the lifespan.

There is ample evidence that more secondary and tertiary education for young people improves their individual life chances. There is also growing evidence, albeit less direct, of a payoff for whole societies from a growth in the proportion of young people gaining qualifications at these levels. But as rapidly changing technology and globalisation transform the pattern of demand for skilled labour throughout the world, raising the proportion of young people who participate in upper secondary or tertiary education can only be part of the solution, for two reasons.

First, because an inflow of better-educated young people will only very gradually change the overall educational level, if not the skill level, of the existing workforce.

Second, because educational attainment, as measured by qualifications, is only one component of human capital. Knowledge and skills continue to be created throughout people's lives, in the non-formal contexts of experiences gained in daily life and at work, as well as within formal educational settings. There is a growing demand in the workplace and elsewhere for individuals who are good at using knowledge flexibly and who can work effectively in teams. These abilities can partly be acquired through education, but must also be developed in the settings where they will be used. So strategies for lifelong learning must look beyond mainstream educational institutions, to ensure that investment in human capital comes to fruition (OECD, 1996a).

2.2 THE PAYOFF OF GREATER EDUCATIONAL ATTAINMENT

An imperfect proxy for human capital

The most frequently used measure of human capital is educational attainment. The average number of years of schooling of the adult population or the proportion of adults who have reached at least a specified educational level are proxy measures of the accumulated stock of human capital. These measures are imperfect, partly because formal education is not the only means of acquiring knowledge and skills, and partly because skills can deteriorate if they are not exercised, and lose value if they are not updated.

Despite such imperfections, evidence tends to support the view that educational attainment does have a close relationship with certain adult competencies, even when they are measured independently of tests used to monitor achievement within formal education. The International Adult Literacy Survey (OECD and Statistics Canada, 1995, and Chapter 3 in this volume) has tested literacy skills in relation to the ability to perform real-life tasks, rather than in relation to any educational curriculum. Its results show that in every country, higher levels of education greatly increase adults' chances of acquiring useful skills. In the first seven OECD countries to undertake the survey, adults without upper secondary education were between two and four times as likely as university graduates to perform at the bottom two

Figure 2.1a
Education and women's employment
Percentage of women aged 30-44 in employment, by level of educational attainment, 1995

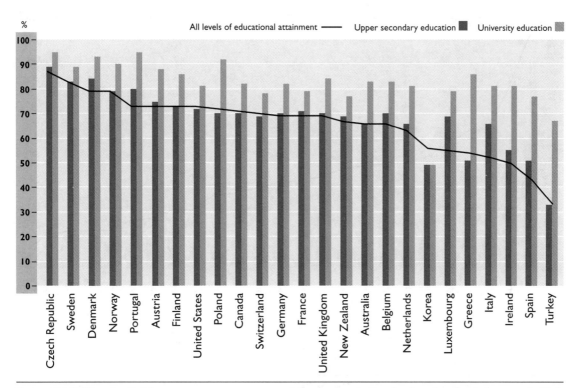

All levels of educational attainment —— Upper secondary education ■ University education ■

Source: OECD Education Database.
Data for Figure 2.1a: page 101.

The great majority of university-educated women in their thirties and early forties are employed, even in countries where overall female employment rates are low.

Countries are ranked by the overall percentage of women in employment.

of five literacy levels. The link was far from perfect: educational attainment was shown neither to be strictly necessary for high literacy performance (19 per cent of less-educated Swedes performed at the top two levels) nor by any means sufficient (27 per cent of high school graduates in the United States were at the bottom two levels). Nevertheless, the strong correlation between educational attainment and adult literacy supports the case for using an expansion in the formal education system as at least one instrument for raising the stock of human capital.

Benefits for individuals

Human capital acquired through formal education has measurable value in terms of economic and social outcomes. The benefits that are easiest to quantify are those accruing to individuals. More

education raises the chances of being employed. It also raises prospective lifetime earnings. These relationships are shown in Figures 2.1 and 2.2.

Two examples of the strong link between education and employment are shown in Figure 2.1. The first example, shown in Figure 2.1a, looks at the proportion of women in mid-life who are in employment, according to their level of initial educational attainment. The focus of this comparison is the population aged 30-44 years. This encompasses a narrow age-band of adults, most of whom have completed full-time education, and who have more similar experiences of work than a wider age-range. The case of women is of particular interest, since their participation in the labour market varies so widely between countries and educational groups.

Figure 2.1b

Education and unemployment
Unemployment rates, ages 30-44, by level of educational attainment, 1995

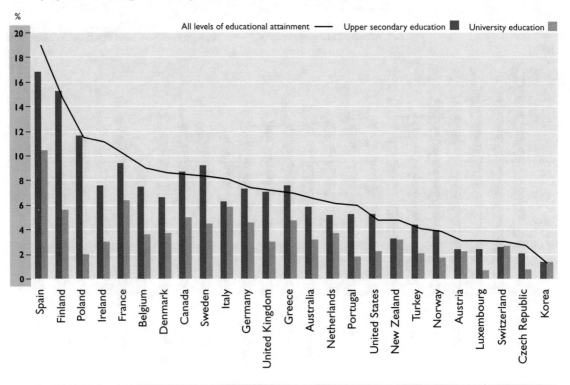

Source: OECD Education Database.

Data for Figure 2.1b: page 101.

University-educated people in their thirties and early forties are up to five times less likely to be unemployed than the average person in that age range. This educational advantage exists everywhere, except in a few countries with very low overall unemployment.

Countries are ranked according to overall unemployment.

The data in Figure 2.1a indicate that in all countries (except Korea), employment rates are higher for those with tertiary-level education than for those with lower attainment (this is the case for both men and women). In some countries there is a particularly wide gap between women's employment rates for those with and without university education. This gap is greatest in countries where relatively few women work overall, as indicated by the line crossing the graph. In these countries, women with university education have a similar chance of working as women with similar qualifications elsewhere: over three-quarters of university-educated women in mid-life are working, in all countries except Korea and Turkey. However, this similarity disappears for women with only upper secondary education: in countries with low overall female participation, this group's

chance of being in employment is also low. Notable examples are Ireland, Greece and Spain, where around half are in employment, compared to between 77 per cent and 86 per cent of women with university qualifications.

Figure 2.1b shows the relationship between unemployment and educational attainment, for adults aged 30-44. Unemployment rates are considerably reduced for university graduates. However, in most countries the unemployment rate for women is much higher than for men at each level of education (for data, see Table E2.1b, Indicator E2 in OECD, 1997). As with the chances of being in employment, the chance of being without work is especially high for women without a full cycle of secondary education. Failure to get a high school diploma and even a post-secondary

Figure 2.2
Education and earnings
Relative mean earnings of women and men aged 30-44, by level of educational attainment, 1995:
Earnings of those with upper secondary education only = 100

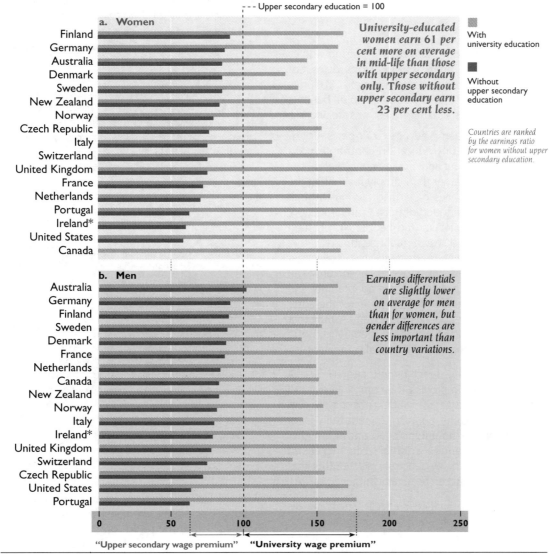

- - - Upper secondary education = 100

a. Women

Finland
Germany
Australia
Denmark
Sweden
New Zealand
Norway
Czech Republic
Italy
Switzerland
United Kingdom
France
Netherlands
Portugal
Ireland*
United States
Canada

*University-educated
women earn 61 per
cent more on average
in mid-life than those
with upper secondary
only. Those without
upper secondary earn
23 per cent less.*

With
university education

Without
upper secondary
education

*Countries are ranked
by the earnings ratio
for women without upper
secondary education.*

b. Men

Australia
Germany
Finland
Sweden
Denmark
France
Netherlands
Canada
New Zealand
Norway
Italy
Ireland*
United Kingdom
Switzerland
Czech Republic
United States
Portugal

*Earnings differentials
are slightly lower
on average for men
than for women, but
gender differences are
less important than
country variations.*

0   50   100   150   200   250

"Upper secondary wage premium"   **"University wage premium"**

* Data refer to 1994.
Source: OECD Education Database.

Data for Figure 2.2: page 102.

qualification appears to create a particular labour market disadvantage for women.

Figure 2.2 shows the strong positive correlation between educational attainment and earnings prospects, for women and men in mid-life. Tertiary graduates earn significantly more than upper secondary graduates in all countries. For men, those without upper secondary education earn between 10 and 38 per cent less than those who have completed upper secondary education only, in most countries, although in Australia the average earnings of the two groups is the same. The expected earnings premium conferred by continuing from upper secondary to tertiary level is generally more pronounced than the premium for upper secondary compared to without upper secondary graduation. This suggests that the upper secondary level constitutes a break-point in many countries, beyond which additional education attracts a particularly high reward.

Social benefits

Improving the relative chances of some individuals to obtain additional qualifications does not necessarily bring overall social benefit. To judge the degree to which more human capital benefits society, the answers to three questions are needed:

- Does increasing access to upper secondary and tertiary education contribute positively to output and employment levels in the aggregate, rather than simply reshuffling the relative chances of individuals? Although education undoubtedly has a "filter" function, helping employers find people with certain desirable and scarce qualities, this is not its only role. High productivity in a knowledge-oriented economy depends on workers at all levels having skills such as adaptability and the ability to learn. The results of the adult literacy survey quoted above demonstrate that more education improves the chances of a worker having relevant general competencies.

- What are the direct benefits to society of individuals improving their employment and earnings prospects, including not only the sum of private gains, but also the reduced cost of supporting the unemployed and the higher public revenues arising from increased earnings? The evidence shows that this kind of social gain can be significant (see Box 2A).

- What are the "spill-over" effects of higher levels of education for some people on the economic and social well-being of other members of a society? Such effects include improved health of the economy and its consequences for overall job creation and growth. Other "externalities" could include social improvements such as improved public health, reduced social disorder, and other possible effects of a reduction in the number of people whose low levels of education give them multiple disadvantages. These kinds of benefits are extremely difficult to quantify, but at a political level create a strong case for investing in human capital.

Box 2A
INDIVIDUAL AND SOCIAL RATES OF RETURN

Attempts to measure the "social" benefits of education and to set them against the cost of the investment have so far yielded very limited results. Evidence from a cross-country study conducted by Psacharopolous (1994) indicates that the measurable social rate of return tends to be about the same as the private rate at the upper secondary level for developed countries. However, at the tertiary level, where public investment tends to be greater, social returns are lower than private rates of return. Psacharopoulos also observed that returns, whether private or social, tend to be lower at tertiary level than at upper secondary level.

It should be borne in mind that no account is taken in these calculations of effects beyond the impact of education on taxes received by public authorities and after-tax earnings of individuals. Omitted impacts such as greater social cohesion, lower crime and better public health – if these could be measured and quantified – may significantly raise the estimated social returns compared with private returns. Nevertheless, the findings highlight the fact that tertiary education costs more to the tax payer, yields more benefit to individuals and recoups less for the public purse relative to its cost than upper secondary education. Prima facie, this creates a case for increasing the contribution to tertiary education made by individual beneficiaries (see also OECD, 1996a, Chapter 8).

Costs and rates of return

Whether for individuals or for societies, the costs of education need to be considered alongside its benefits before the return on investment can be calculated. From the individual's point of view, cost corresponds to the direct costs of tuition (e.g. fees), educational materials, and forgone earnings. Social costs include all of private costs as well as those direct costs incurred by public authorities in providing for education. If the total social cost of graduation is taken into account, a rate of return can be estimated by comparing this cost with the additional lifetime earnings associated with graduation at that level. This is a hybrid between an individual and a social rate of return, since it looks at social costs but does not measure social

Figure 2.3
Rates of return to education
Estimated rates of return to university and upper secondary education, over a working lifetime,
for women and men, 1995

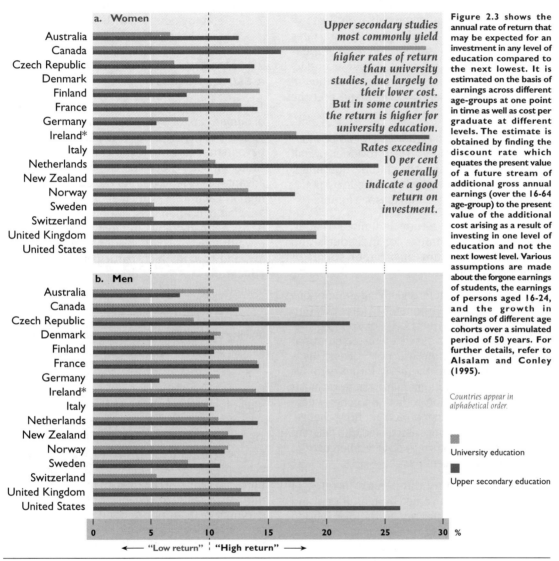

Figure 2.3 shows the annual rate of return that may be expected for an investment in any level of education compared to the next lowest. It is estimated on the basis of earnings across different age-groups at one point in time as well as cost per graduate at different levels. The estimate is obtained by finding the discount rate which equates the present value of a future stream of additional gross annual earnings (over the 16-64 age-group) to the present value of the additional cost arising as a result of investing in one level of education and not the next lowest level. Various assumptions are made about the forgone earnings of students, the earnings of persons aged 16-24, and the growth in earnings of different age cohorts over a simulated period of 50 years. For further details, refer to Alsalam and Conley (1995).

Countries appear in alphabetical order.

■ University education

■ Upper secondary education

* Data refer to 1994.
Source: OECD Education Database.

Data for Figure 2.3: page 102.

benefits beyond the gross earnings accruing to individuals. But it does give some indication about whether investment in education is worthwhile. For example, a rate of return of 10 per cent could be treated as a "threshold" rate above which return on an investment is viewed as potentially being worth making compared to alternative investments.

The results shown in Figure 2.3 indicate that annual rates of return for upper secondary level are generally high (typically above 10 per cent) for both men and women. Rates of return on tertiary education tend to be slightly lower on average than rates on upper secondary. In the case of seven countries, the rates for university education fall below 10 per cent for women, with particularly low returns in Italy, Sweden and Switzerland. So even though earnings at tertiary level relative to upper secondary are higher than is the case for upper secondary relative to lower secondary education, when the high costs of university education are taken into account, rates of return at upper secondary level appear relatively high. High returns on upper secondary graduation are obtained by women and men in Ireland, the Netherlands, Switzerland and the United States.

The data presented in Figure 2.3 should be interpreted with some caution. They provide an overall picture of broad orders of magnitude, but cannot be treated as precise estimates or guides to policy decisions. There are several reasons for this:

- The measure of returns is limited to additional gross earnings for individuals and takes no account of broader social or economic effects.

- The effects of various underlying assumptions in arriving at the estimates of rates of return may be open to question. For example, lifetime earnings across different age-groups at one point in time are not necessarily a reliable guide to the likely future earnings profile of a cohort graduating at a particular level of education today. As general economic and labour market conditions change, the lifetime earnings associated with different educational levels may be very different from those of the recent past.

- Between country differences in rates of return may be governed by institutional and non-market influences on the distribution of earnings – in some European countries, the more compressed wage structure may be less attributable to a more equitable distribution of human capital than to low flexibility in relative earnings.

- Rates of return estimates are based on average earnings and costs. No account is taken of within-country differences in returns for a particular level of education. For example, particular fields of study or particular social groups may experience very different rates of return, even for the same level of education.

- The estimates focus solely on the financial gains arising from education for those in employment. They take no account of the fact that more educational attainment is likely to be associated with a lower risk of unemployment, or with other social and personal benefits.

2.3 RAISING ATTAINMENT LEVELS: A SLOW PROCESS

The most straightforward way of raising the stock of human capital is to increase the proportion of young people who continue to be educated beyond the years when schooling is compulsory. Although such expansion can be expensive, its advantages extend beyond the enhancement of human capital: in particular, it helps meet the growing educational aspirations of the population. A steady move in most OECD countries towards universal participation in upper secondary, and towards high participation in tertiary education, has been driven partly by higher demand for qualifications, partly by governments' decisions to expand provision, and in some cases by extended compulsion: the school leaving age has risen in some countries to as high as 18, if certain types of training options are included (see Chapters 4 and 5).

Despite recent expansion, there remain wide differences in the levels of formal educational attainment of the adult population of various OECD countries. Those lower down this range may be at a disadvantage in the global knowledge economy if they fail to make up this shortfall in human capital. An alternative may be to accept more low-skill, low-wage jobs. But can an expansion in upper secondary and tertiary education for young people be sufficient to close the education gap within a realistic period of time?

Figure 2.4a shows the proportion of adults aged 25-64 with at least upper secondary education in 1995, and the proportion who would be at this level in 2015 if the present rate of graduation were maintained. These projections are not forecasts: it is likely that in most countries graduation rates will go on rising. But they serve as illustrations that put into perspective for policymakers the rate at which the overall stock of human capital would change as a result of

Figure 2.4a
Projected growth in the educational level of the adult population
Percentage of population aged 25-64 having completed upper secondary education, assuming 1995 youth qualification rates

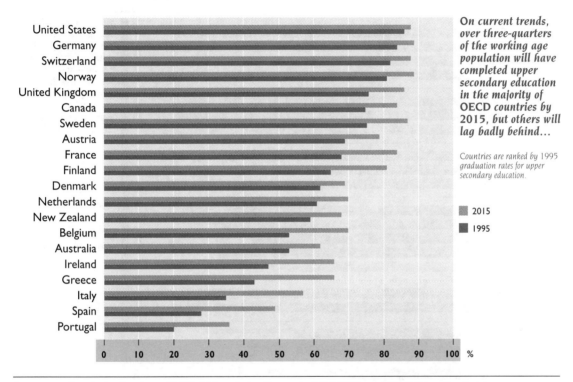

On current trends, over three-quarters of the working age population will have completed upper secondary education in the majority of OECD countries by 2015, but others will lag badly behind...

Countries are ranked by 1995 graduation rates for upper secondary education.

■ 2015
■ 1995

Sources: UN Population Database; UN World Population Prospects (1950-2050); and OECD Education Database.
Data and notes for Figure 2.4a: page 103.

present inflows of young upper secondary graduates. They underline the fact that changes depending on raising the attainment of young people will only be gradual.

At present, more than 80 per cent of the population aged 25-64 years have at least upper secondary education in Germany, Norway, Switzerland and the United States, compared to fewer than one in three adults in Portugal and Spain. These attainment rates result from historic graduation rates: the United States, for example, has high attainment because it universalised high-school access long before most European countries. So today's 40- and 50-year-old workers in the United States are more

likely to have completed a full cycle of secondary education compared with similar workers in Australia, Canada, New Zealand and European countries.

Since many European countries currently have higher rates of upper secondary graduation than the United States, where one quarter of youth fail to obtain a diploma at the theoretical age of upper secondary completion, some catching-up will take place if graduation rates remain at their present levels. This scenario is illustrated in Figure 2.4b. The projection is derived by tracking cohorts in various age-bands and assuming that they do not acquire additional qualifications other than what would be expected

Figure 2.4b
Growth in youth qualification rates needed to accelerate the growth in overall education levels
Proportion of population aged 25-29 required to have completed upper secondary education, for overall adult educational attainment to reach a specified threshold by 2015

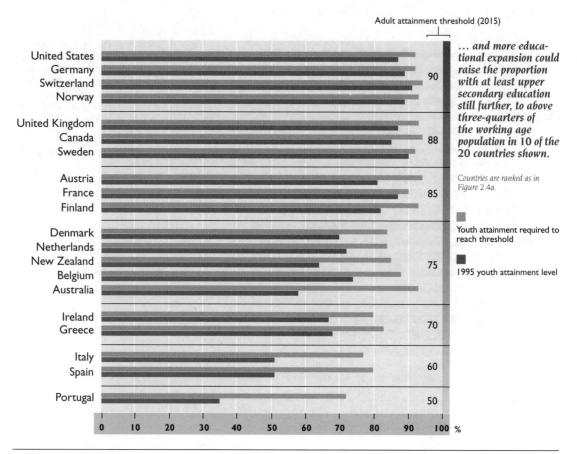

Adult attainment threshold (2015)

... and more educational expansion could raise the proportion with at least upper secondary education still further, to above three-quarters of the working age population in 10 of the 20 countries shown.

Countries are ranked as in Figure 2.4a.

▪ Youth attainment required to reach threshold

▪ 1995 youth attainment level

Sources: UN Population Database; UN World Population Prospects (1950-2050); and OECD Education Database.
Data and notes for Figure 2.4b: page 103.

from current rates of participation in adult education.[1] If graduation rates were to remain at present levels over the next 20 years then the following results would likely emerge:

- The ranking of countries in terms of the level of educational attainment of the adult population would not change much.

- Countries with the lowest attainment levels (Australia, Belgium, Greece, Ireland, Italy, Portugal and Spain) would move nearer to the United States, while roughly retaining their rank.

- Australia, Italy, New Zealand, Portugal and Spain would make the biggest strides, with increases of 20 percentage points or above, in order for them to reach the specified adult attainment threshold in 2015.

In practice, these projections will underestimate the convergence between countries' attainment levels if countries with lower levels

---

1. It involves assuming that migration flows in and out of countries do not substantially alter educational attainment – an assumption which is not always valid for younger cohorts in some OECD countries. Each "incoming" cohort of persons aged 25-29 after 1995 is assumed to have at least the same level of educational attainment of any age-group in 1995.

respond by raising drastically the proportion of young people participating in upper secondary education. There is clearly more limited scope for increases at this level for countries in which the majority of adults already have upper secondary qualifications. Figure 2.4b looks at how much each country would have to raise the attainment of their young people over the next 20 years in order for upper secondary attainment to reach particular levels among the whole adult population. Clearly every country could not have the same target: in some countries in which a minority of young adults have so far completed secondary school, even if every young person did so over the next 20 years, the attainment rate of the whole adult population would not reach the 80 per cent threshold currently seen in Norway and the United States.

So Figure 2.4b looks at potential attainment rates that could conceivably be achieved by countries over the next 20 years, albeit sometimes only with big increases in upper secondary graduation. Portugal, for example, would need a big expansion in upper secondary education just to get a majority of adults to this level by 2015 – 72 per cent of young people would need to qualify during the intervening period, compared to the 35 per cent of 25-29 year-olds who have done so today. At the other extreme, the United States, Norway, Germany and Switzerland could raise overall attainment above 90 per cent with only modest increases in young people's attainment. About half of all countries could reach 85 per cent – around the current level achieved in the United States – with only modest further expansion of upper secondary completion.

These examples are again illustrative rather than constituting forecasts or recommendations. They unrealistically assume a new rate of attainment for 25-29 year-olds, starting immediately. But they do demonstrate the task facing countries seeking to use schooling and initial tertiary education to upgrade the overall knowledge and skills of their population. The results show that the eight countries where adult attainment is below 60 per cent at present still face a big task in raising it to significantly higher levels.

2.4 INVESTMENT OVER THE LIFE-CYCLE

Raising rates of educational attainment among young people is a necessary part of any strategy to improve the supply of human capital, but on its own it will be insufficient. To be effective, learning must be a lifelong enterprise, starting in early childhood when important foundations can be established, affecting future learning habits. As noted in Section 2.1 above, investment needs also to continue into adulthood, both because replenishing the "stock" of human capital by relying on new labour market entrants is too slow and because skills need to be learned and renewed beyond formal education settings in order to be effective. But even for adults, learning inside and outside educational institutions are not alternatives: they can be complementary.

The effectiveness of such learning will depend on a variety of decisions taken by individuals and organisations; in many cases these are beyond the control of governments. It is difficult to measure the extent and quality of learning outside formal education because of the variety of settings in which it occurs. But governments can take a particular interest in two ways of increasing the stock of human capital beyond the lengthening of young people's initial studies. First, adult learning can add to the overall level of educational attainment. Second, work-related education and training can build employee skills through a mixture of on-the-job training and separate study.

Contribution of adult learning to overall educational attainment

The results shown previously in Figure 2.4b illustrate the difficulty of raising educational attainment levels solely by increasing participation among today's youth cohorts. Countries that want to upgrade attainment more quickly can also aim to do so by expanding adult education. This is likely to be a strategy employed by countries with low levels of attainment, particularly those where youth participation rates have recently risen sharply. In such cases, without adult education, a wide disparity will open up between highly-qualified younger generations and unqualified older ones. This was the position of Norway and Sweden after their rapid

Figure 2.5
Adult participation in education and training
Percentage of population aged 26-65 who participated in education or training,
classified by main programme undertaken, 1994[1]

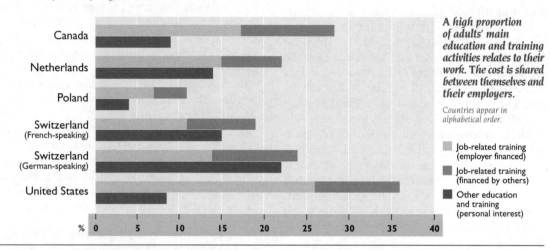

A *high proportion
of adults' main
education and training
activities relates to their
work. The cost is shared
between themselves and
their employers.*

*Countries appear in
alphabetical order.*

Job-related training
(employer financed)

Job-related training
(financed by others)

Other education
and training
(personal interest)

1. The data refer to the percentage of the adult population aged 26-65 which participated in at least one training programme during the 12 months prior to the survey. The distinction between participation in employer-financed training and other types of education or training is made on the basis of the *main* training programme taken by individuals during the 12 months preceding the interview (there being more than one programme per individual in some cases).
Source: OECD and Statistics Canada, International Adult Literacy Survey.
Data and notes for Figure 2.5: page 104.

expansion during the 1970s, when they opened up "second chance" education for adults to an unprecedented level. Such strategies may suit some Southern European countries today.

In thinking about the degree to which educational attainment can be topped up in adulthood, however, the distinction between first and second chances may be becoming less relevant. Traditionally, tertiary education has tended to follow immediately on the completion of upper secondary schooling. The duration of studies has been growing, as students take longer to complete them, or have topped up "initial" tertiary education with additional degrees or qualifications (see Chapter 5). But the prolonging of the period of full transition to the labour market also involves more flexible interspersion of studies and work, that may combine part-time study, distance learning and "sandwich" courses. A large range of education and training options could be developed with more flexibility in attendance and entry requirements. In this way, various types of post-secondary education can

occur recurrently over the course of a working lifetime in a way more suited to individual needs, both job-related and otherwise (OECD, 1973). More flexibility in post-secondary provision may also have the effect of lowering unit costs and allowing a greater number of people to participate within public funding constraints.

Encouraging job-related education and training

Policy-makers can have some influence over job-related education and training, both by encouraging enterprises to invest in the skills of their workers and by maximising the effectiveness of public labour market training programmes.

Figure 2.5 shows the extent of engagement of the population aged 26-65 in various types of adult education and training offerings in five of the countries that participated in the International Adult Literacy Survey in 1994. For the countries shown, the majority of adults who participated in any form of organised education or training

Table 2.1
On-the-job training, productivity and earnings
Selected research findings on the impact of employer-sponsored training on employee productivity and earnings

Country	Study	Data	Definition and scope of training	Conclusions
Netherlands	Groot (1994)	Survey among employers about training for workers	Enterprise-related training	On average training increases productivity by 16% and wages by 12%
United Kingdom	Groot and Oosterbeek (1995)	Employees in 1991; data taken from the Household Panel Survey	Training that was part of present employment and any other training during the past year	On-the-job training increases wages by 15%
United States	Bishop (1994)	Data on young male hires at low wages (firm level); Employment Opportunity Pilot Project Survey	Training during the first three months of employment	Formal training by previous employers increased initial productivity by 9.5% but had no effect on wages
United States	Black and Lynch (1996)	Sample of establishments (manufacturing and non-manufacturing, private sector)	Formal training - Total number of workers who received (formal) training - % of training that occurred off the job - Contents of training	Training has an ambiguous impact on the value of sales (the proxy for productivity) of establishments. In both manufacturing and non-manufacturing, the number of workers trained has no apparent impact on output (sales) when controlling for other inputs (capital, material, hours worked). The content of the training programme seems to be more important
France	Laulhé (1990)	Employees aged 15 and over in 1985. Survey of Professional Qualifications Training	Employer-sponsored training	Persons who received some training were much less likely to go from employment to unemployment and more likely to experience occupational mobility

linked these activities to work – even though non-workers were included in the sample. Only in Switzerland (German-speaking) was the number reporting a connection with work (24 per cent) close to the number reporting no connection (22 per cent).

The proportion of the adult population participating in job-related training varies from 11 per cent in Poland to 36 per cent in the United States. Such training is often subsidised by employers, but a surprisingly high share in the total cost of such training comes from other sources. In the case of Canada, German-speaking Switzerland, and the United States, approximately 10 per cent of all adults participated in some form of job-related training over the previous year without receiving any financial contribution from their employers.

Evidence from both IALS and data collected by means of labour force surveys (see Figure 3.4, Chapter 3, this volume) show that participation in job-related training in the employed adult population is correlated with educational attainment. This implies that access to training for adults is unequal and that those at lower levels of educational attainment have either less incentive or less opportunity to engage in training throughout their working lives. The disadvantage thus created may well be cumulative over a working life-time.

It is likely that firm-specific training entails a payoff to both individuals and sponsoring employers, which justifies the investment. Various studies have shown that adult education and training adapted to individual learner needs and linked to on-the-job training schemes have beneficial effects on productivity, earnings and job tenure. Table 2.1 presents a summary of key findings obtained in several research studies for selected countries.

But what role should public labour market programmes play in supplementing employer-sponsored training? The evidence for the effectiveness of such programmes is inconclusive.

Evaluations to date (OECD, 1993; OECD, 1996*b*) have indicated low or insignificant returns to public labour market training programmes in a wide range of OECD countries. However, a number of caveats are needed. Evaluation of outcomes from such training needs to be of sufficiently long duration to allow for effects to be properly measured. Also, externalities such as lower crime incidence and better health are typically not accounted for in the evaluations. It appears that some types of training programme, particularly those more adapted to individual trainee as well as employer needs, work better.

The content, duration and certification of training are important issues. For some groups, especially young people and women re-entering the labour force, formal classroom instruction is in many cases effective. One should not expect large returns when expenditures for such training are limited (Lalonde, 1995). Given that the amount invested is still relatively low per participant, to expect it to raise earnings by a large amount would imply an extremely large rate of return. It is therefore difficult to generalise from evaluations of specific schemes for specific groups to public labour market training in general. A better targeting of interventions and types of training is more pertinent than a consideration of the merits of such training vis-à-vis longer and more formal types of education or training.

The solution may be to combine such training with formal education through, for example, alternating periods of on-the-job training and study accompanied by formal certification. This, however, raises the issue of who pays for an expansion of training. It is not evident that employers are prepared to invest heavily if the gains are not tangible or appropriated directly by enterprises. In this sense, the well-known "market failure" and "poaching" problems arise: Employers may have a reason to under-invest in training because other companies may poach trained workers or because the benefits of such training to individual and company productivity are not apparent. Thus, there is a need to re-orientate wage-bargaining and human resource management towards a system of rewarding skills, competencies and human capital investment. There is also a need to achieve greater transparency about the investment pay-off to training and the value of workforce skills.

2.5 CONCLUSIONS

Although indicators of the size and effectiveness of human capital investment are incomplete and approximate, they can provide some guidance to policy-makers over priorities and goals. One challenge facing policy-makers today is to direct resources into learning pathways which yield the best value for money. Another is to bring about more equitable opportunities to learn. Access to tertiary and adult education in many countries remains socially imbalanced, partly because of underlying inequalities in the learning opportunities encountered earlier in life.

So strategies for enhancing human capital formation through lifelong learning cannot simply concentrate on continuing the expansion of provision and participation in education immediately after the school leaving age. They must start before this stage and finish well after it. Early childhood education and intervention programmes in primary school are important elements in bringing about more equal opportunities in foundation learning and assisting children at risk. Learning pathways that start at school need to be continued throughout adulthood.

One such pathway discussed in this chapter is to combine on-the-job training and formal study. Where resources are limited, it is important to look at cost-effective options such as part-time studies, distance learning and modular programmes adapted to individual learning interests, needs and circumstances. Small amounts of public resources invested in such programmes can often help leverage private investments from employers and individuals. The considerable economic benefits accruing to students, particularly of tertiary education, point to the desirability of individuals making some contribution to the cost where feasible.

Education and training cannot on their own cure unemployment or other social ills – other ingredients have to be brought to bear, including labour market and social reforms as well as macro-economic policy. However, the cost of not investing in human capital can be great. It exposes countries to the risk of entrenched unemployment, greater social exclusion, a mismatch of job skills and a loss of economic opportunity. ■

References

ALSALAM, N. and **CONLEY, R**. (1995), "The rate of return to education: A proposal for an indicator", *Education and Employment*, OECD, Paris.

BISHOP, J. (1994), "The impact of productivity on wages", in L.M. Lynch (ed.), *Training and the Private Sector: International Comparisons*, University of Chicago Press, Chicago, Illinois.

BLACK, S.E. and **LYNCH, L.M.** (1996), "Human capital investments and productivity", *American Economic Research*, Papers and Proceedings, May.

GROOT, W. (1994), "Bedrijfsopleidingen goed voor loon en produktiviteit", *Economisch Statistische Berichten*, No. 3988, pp. 1108-1111.

GROOT, W. and **OOSTERBEEK, H.** (1995), "Determinants and wage effects of different components of participation in on- and off-the-job training", *Research Memorandum*, Tinbergen Institute, Rotterdam.

LALONDE, R.J. (1995), "The promise of public sector-sponsored training programs", *Journal of Economic Perspectives*, Vol. 9 (2), pp. 149-169.

LAULHÉ, P. (1990), "La formation continue : un avantage pour les promotions et un accès privilégié pour les jeunes et les techniciens", *Economie et Statistique*, No. 228, pp. 3-8.

OECD (1973), *Recurrent Education: A Strategy for Lifelong Learning*, Centre for Educational Research and Innovation, Paris.

OECD (1993), *Employment Outlook*, Paris.

OECD (1996a), *Lifelong Learning for All*, Paris.

OECD (1996b), "Enhancing the effectiveness of active labour market policies: Evidence from programme evaluations in OECD countries", Labour Market and Social Policy Occasional Papers, No. 18, Paris.

OECD (1997), *Education at a Glance: OECD Indicators*, Paris.

OECD and **STATISTICS CANADA** (1995), *Literacy, Economy and Society: Results of the First International Adult Literacy Survey*, Paris and Ottawa.

PSACHAROPOULOS, G. (1994), "Returns to investment in education: A global update", *World Development*, Vol. 22 (9), pp. 1325-1343.

CHAPTER 3

LITERACY SKILLS: USE THEM OR LOSE THEM

SUMMARY

This chapter draws on some of the main findings of the International Adult Literacy Survey (IALS), which has taken an important first step towards measuring directly the stock of basic skills in the adult population. By 1997, results are available for 12 countries.

The survey has drawn attention to a much greater than expected adult literacy problem in OECD countries. It has also contributed new insights into the nature of literacy that are crucial for developing policy strategies. This chapter emphasises that literacy is "organic" in character: it develops and changes over the life-span, rather than simply being acquired in youth and kept for life, like a university degree or the ability to ride a bicycle. Literacy skills must be maintained and developed further through active use. This raises three issues that create challenges for policy-makers – beyond their traditional engagement with the educational attainment of youth:

- How much do adults use their literacy skills in the workplace, and does this influence performance? The evidence indicates that among blue-collar workers in particular, there is an untapped pool of talent, which could be lost if it is not better used through changes in work practices.

- How much do adults use their literacy skills in daily activities at home and in the community, and how does this relate to their literacy levels? The evidence shows wide variations from one country to another, but in general, a lower engagement in literacy practices outside rather than inside work, with a particular slant towards better-educated groups who have adequate reading materials in the home.

- How can employers and communities help to create a culture of literacy and lifelong learning? Employers have a greater potential role than previously thought, because of the importance of the work context to much adult learning. The way in which work is organised, and the incentives for workers to upgrade their skills, are two key features that need improving. Policy change will therefore need to involve a partnership between governments, employers and individuals that seeks to promote a literacy-rich work culture.

3.1 INTRODUCTION

Across the OECD there is a new concern with the demand and supply of adult basic skills. Although the specific vocabulary that is used differs among countries – variously called "foundation skills", "essential" or "necessary" skills, "key competencies" or "start qualifications", depending on the country, there is widespread agreement on the centrality of literacy and numeracy skills. They are seen everywhere as the foundation on which the acquisition and development of other, often job-specific competencies critically depends.

Globalisation and technological change are the twin driving forces behind the growing concern with the skill base of the adult population. Until now shifts that impacted on the comparative advantage of nations tended to occur only gradually. The future was to an extent predictable, and this was reflected in both economic and education policies. But the global knowledge economy has changed that. Innovations leading to changing skill requirements occur more frequently and more quickly. Global competition encourages more rapid diffusion, thanks to the widespread deployment of information and communication technologies, reduced barriers to trade and investment, and the near-instantaneous flow of financial capital. To an even larger extent than before, governments must therefore rely on the creativity, flexibility and adaptability of individuals, businesses and communities. But all these qualities depend first and foremost on the competencies of the population. Literacy is key to a skilled and adaptable work force, which in turn is a major determinant of continued economic prosperity, democracy and social cohesion.

Before the publication in the early 1990s of a series of influential reports in North America and by the OECD,[1] low adult literacy was considered by some as a problem mainly for developing countries. This was in part because there had been no way of measuring literacy skills directly, so proxy measures – such as the percentage of the population with at most four years of primary schooling – were commonly used to estimate literacy rates. By this minimal education standard, and according to UNESCO statistics, over 95 per cent of citizens living in most OECD countries were classified as "literate". In this approach literacy was seen as a dichotomous attribute: one was either "literate" or "illiterate", and the cut-off depended on whether one had received a few years of formal schooling.

The new approaches to measurement pioneered in North America[2] recognise that the emerging knowledge society has changed both expectations and demands, and that literacy skill requirements have increased, by some measures dramatically so. In the new perspective, literacy is seen not as a minimum level of reading ability mastered at school by almost all those growing up in developed countries. Educational attainment, by itself, is considered an inadequate proxy measure, because literacy skills once acquired in school can deteriorate rapidly if not used in the post-education years, and because such skills can be acquired and improved later on, even independently of the training programmes organised by adult education institutions. Because literacy is a "moving target", a single cut-off in terms of "literates" and "illiterates" cannot meaningfully be set. For the purposes of recent surveys and throughout this chapter, the term "literacy" is instead used to refer to a particular skill – namely the ability to understand and employ printed information in daily activities, at home, at work and in the community – and its usage in order to achieve one's goals, and to develop one's knowledge and potential. Thus a much more complex picture of literacy emerges, one of individuals placed along a continuum of ability.

The above definition provided the basis for the first International Adult Literacy Survey (IALS) undertaken by seven OECD countries in the

---

1.   See Kirsch *et al.* (1993); Montigny, Kelly and Jones (1991). See also *Adult Illiteracy and Economic Performance* (OECD, 1992), *Literacy, Economy and Society* (OECD and Statistics Canada, 1995) and *Literacy Skills for the Knowledge Society* (OECD and Statistics Canada, 1997). Also of interest is Wickert (1989).

2.   See Murray, Kirsch and Jenkins (1997), and Tuijnman, Kirsch and Wagner (1997), for an explanation of the new approaches to measurement and the policy issues they give rise to.

autumn of 1994, using a representative sample of the adult population aged 16-65. Five additional countries took part in the assessment in 1995, applying the same methodology. The respondents were interviewed for about 20 minutes and then took a 45-minute literacy skill test in their homes in their national languages. This test, which was developed under the supervision of Statistics Canada and the Educational Testing Service in the United States, required participants to perform tasks based on everyday situations, of varying levels of difficulty. Box 3A explains how literacy proficiency was measured and how the results can be interpreted.

Box 3A
HOW TO INTERPRET THE SURVEY RESULTS?

The survey assessed literacy proficiency in terms of three domains, each encompassing a common set of skills relevant for diverse tasks:

- *Prose literacy* – the knowledge and skills needed to understand and use information from printed texts including editorials, new stories, poems and fiction.

- *Document literacy* – the knowledge and skills required to locate and use information contained in various formats, including job applications, payroll forms, transportation schedules, maps, tables and charts.

- *Quantitative literacy* – the knowledge and skills required to apply arithmetic operations, either alone or sequentially, to numbers embedded in printed materials, such as balancing a cheque-book, figuring out a tip, completing an order form or determining the amount of interest on a loan from an advertisement.

All 101 common test items used for the assessment were open-ended and taken from "real-life" stimuli; they reflect the literacy requirements encountered in everyday life. In each of the three domains a scale was constructed, upon which tasks of varying difficulty were placed. A person's literacy ability was then expressed by a score in each domain, defined as the point on the scale at which he or she had an 80 per cent chance of successfully performing a given task. The data collection, scoring and scaling methodology is explained in detail in Murray *et al.* (1997).

For analytical purposes, the ranges of scores achieved were grouped into five proficiency levels, reflecting the empirically determined progression of information-processing skills and strategies:

Level 1 (0-225 points) indicates persons with very poor literacy skills;

Level 2 (226-275 points) identifies individuals who although they can read can deal only with material that is simple, clearly laid out, and in which the tasks involved are not too complex;

Level 3 (276-325 points) denotes people with the ability to integrate several sources of information and solve more complex problems. This is the level of skill regarded by many experts as a suitable minimum for coping with the demands of everyday life and work in a modern society.

Levels 4-5 (326-500 points) describe respondents who demonstrate the capacity to use higher order thinking and information-processing skills. Since the numbers performing at the highest skill level are small (under five per cent in most countries), Levels 4 and 5 are combined for the purposes of the data analysis.

Figure 3.1
Comparative distributions of literacy proficiency on three scales
Proportion of population aged 16-65 who are at a particular literacy level,
relative to the Level 3 baseline, 1994-1995

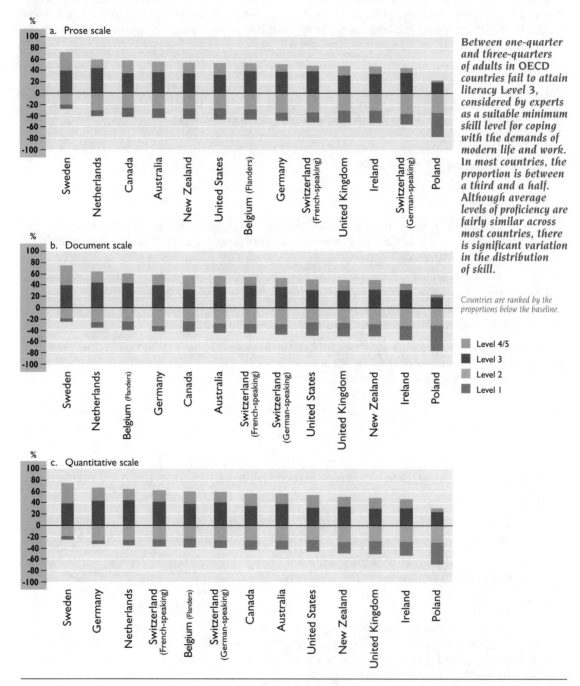

Between one-quarter and three-quarters of adults in OECD countries fail to attain literacy Level 3, considered by experts as a suitable minimum skill level for coping with the demands of modern life and work. In most countries, the proportion is between a third and a half. Although average levels of proficiency are fairly similar across most countries, there is significant variation in the distribution of skill.

Countries are ranked by the proportions below the baseline.

Level 4/5
Level 3
Level 2
Level 1

Source: OECD and Statistics Canada, International Adult Literacy Survey.
Data for Figure 3.1: page 105.

3.2 LOW LITERACY IS A PROBLEM EVERYWHERE

The International Adult Literacy Survey shows that there is little discernible difference between the overall or mean literacy level of adults in the majority of the countries that took part. Swedish adults significantly outperform similar populations in the other countries in all three literacy domains (see Box 3A), whereas adults in Poland perform worse. But the mean scores in the other countries – Australia, Belgium (Flanders[3]), Canada, Germany, Ireland, the Netherlands, New Zealand, Switzerland (German and French-speaking cantons), the United Kingdom and the United States – were too close together to be statistically significant with the sample sizes used. However, in some cases the results were different according to the type of literacy measured. For example, the Netherlands does better in prose literacy and less well in quantitative literacy than does Germany; United States adults perform similarly to Canadians in both prose and quantitative literacy, but less well in document literacy; and Swiss adults perform better on quantitative than prose reading tasks.

But even though the mean performance levels are similar for most of the countries that took part in the study, there is considerable variation in the distribution of literacy skills in the population. The distribution of literacy can be as important an indicator of a country's potential economic and social strengths as the mean performance level. For example, a workforce with a high mean literacy level that is skewed towards exceptional achievement among a minority may fare worse than one where literacy is somewhat lower on average, but more evenly distributed, with fewer people on the lowest level.

Differences among countries in the distribution of literacy skills in the adult population aged 16-65 are indicated in Figures 3.1a-c. The graphs show, for each of the three scales, what percentage of adults scored at each of the five levels. To help compare the distribution, the bars show what percentage of the population score at level three or above, and what percentage only reach Levels 1 or 2. Level 3 is considered by

experts as a suitable minimum for coping with the complex demands of life and work in the knowledge society.

There are large proportions of people in Levels 1 and 2 in all the countries. Even Swedish policy-makers are concerned that one-quarter of the population falls into the two lowest levels on the three IALS scales. For the other countries, the proportion ranges from between one-third in Germany and the Netherlands to just over one-half in Ireland and the United Kingdom. For Poland, it is three-quarters.

In some countries, there is also serious cause for concern over the high proportion with very low literacy skills, who score at Level 1. In Ireland, New Zealand, the United Kingdom and the United States, close to one-quarter of the adult population scores at this level on the document scale. The comparable figures are 17 per cent for Australia, 15 per cent for Belgium (Flanders), 18 per cent for Canada, 9 per cent for Germany, 10 per cent for the Netherlands, and 16 to 18 per cent for French- and German-speaking Switzerland. There is a particularly wide range on the quantitative scale, where one in 16 Germans but nearly one in four Irish and UK adults are at Level 1. Thus, although low literacy is a serious condition in all countries, there are significant differences in how literacy is distributed, and these differences are likely to matter both economically and socially.

Objective evidence indicates not only that there is a large group of people with low skills in the OECD area, but that this lack of skill makes it difficult for some groups to participate fully in economic life. Low literacy is associated with higher unemployment incidence and a more frequent reliance on social assistance (see Figure 4.5). In addition, Figure 3.2 shows the relationship between earnings from work and prose and quantitative literacy for the employed population aged 25-65. The premium on skill is significant in all countries, but particularly high in

---

3. The Belgium IALS-sample is representative of the "Flemish Region", excluding Brussels. Therefore, the name Flanders is used throughout this chapter, rather than "Flemish Community".

Figure 3.2

Relative effect of literacy on earnings

Proportion of employed people aged 25-65 at each literacy level who are in the top 60 per cent of earners: percentage points difference from Level 3, 1994-1995

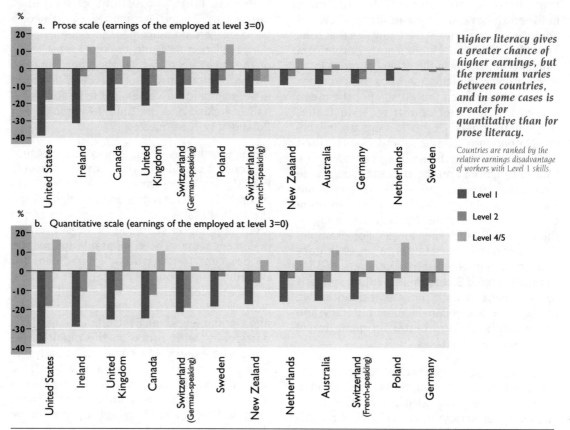

Higher literacy gives a greater chance of higher earnings, but the premium varies between countries, and in some cases is greater for quantitative than for prose literacy.

Countries are ranked by the relative earnings disadvantage of workers with Level 1 skills.

■ Level 1
■ Level 2
■ Level 4/5

Source: OECD and Statistics Canada, International Adult Literacy Survey.

Data for Figure 3.2: page 106.

Canada, Ireland, the United Kingdom and the United States. Smaller wage premia are observed in Australia, Germany, the Netherlands, New Zealand and Poland. It is of interest to note that whereas in some countries there is a similar wage premium from different types of literacy skills, the labour market appears to reward quantitative skills more than prose reading skills in Australia, the Netherlands, Sweden, the United Kingdom and the United States.

3.3 LITERACY IS NOT LIKE RIDING A BICYCLE

Can policy-makers realistically hope to address deficiencies in adult literacy by strengthening the quality of early schooling and generally continuing to expand enrolments in post-compulsory education? The IALS results indicate that while improved schooling is part of the answer, it is not a sufficient response because the literacy skills of young persons leaving formal education can rise or fall subsequently, depending on learning experience on and off the job during adulthood.

Figure 3.3 shows the mean proficiency score in each country for successive levels of education on the quantitative scale. There is a strong relationship between educational attainment and quantitative literacy, but it is not a definitive connection. Low educated adults in the age group 25 to 65 perform on average much worse than highly educated people. In all countries

Figure 3.3
Mean literacy score by educational attainment
Mean score on quantitative scale with range of 0-500 points of adults aged 25-65 by highest completed level of education, 1994-1995

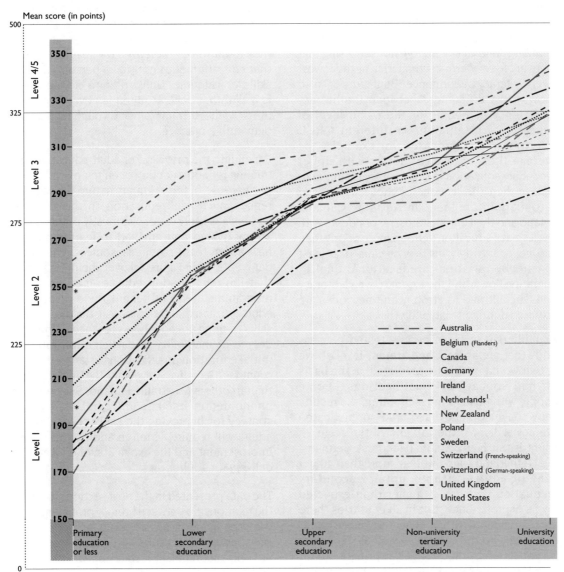

Better educated adults have higher literacy on average. But adults with similar educational attainment have greatly differing average literacy scores in different countries.

The chart shows the gradients for the countries.

* Unreliable estimate.
1. The category non-university tertiary education does not apply.
Source: OECD and Statistics Canada, International Adult Literacy Survey.
Data for Figure 3.3: page 106.

studied, adults without a full cycle of secondary education are predominantly at Levels 1 and 2, and those with some tertiary education experience are predominantly at Levels 3 to 5. For example, 55 per cent of the Irish adult population has not completed a full cycle of secondary education, compared with only 16 per cent of German adults. It is therefore not surprising that there are fewer Germans than Irish at the lowest level of literacy performance. But Figure 3.3 also shows large differences between the literacy proficiency of people at the same level of educational attainment in different OECD countries. In some cases, for example, the average literacy level of adults with upper secondary education in one country is similar to or less than the average of those with lower secondary in another. In Autralia, Canada, Poland and the United States, respondents with low levels of education perform more poorly than in other countries. This may be caused, at least in part, by variation in educational quality, migration flows, and the extent to which literacy skills are allowed to atrophy and new ones are acquired during life beyond school.

Roughly one in three people tested possess skills that are at least one literacy level above or below what would be predicted on the basis of their educational qualifications. Some people with little formal schooling, the results show, have somehow acquired sophisticated literacy skills. At the top end of the scale, in countries such as Belgium (Flanders), Germany, the Netherlands and Sweden, more than 40 per cent of adults without upper secondary graduation perform at higher than expected levels of proficiency. But in all countries there are respondents with relatively advanced qualifications who did not do as well as expected. So education is important as a springboard for developing literacy skills, but it is not the sole determinant. Literacy skills are obtained in a variety of ways, and some of these do not depend on the school system. The key to the design of successful intervention strategies thus lies in understanding the mechanisms through which people maintain and update their skills, for example through workplace learning, life experience or simply personal initiative.

Expanding education systems and improving quality will make a big difference in the long term. But clearly, given that there are large proportions of people over 45 with low levels of initial schooling, it will be many years before more highly educated young cohorts have replaced the on average lower-educated older age groups in the labour force. Moreover, the results suggest that education does not "fix" a person's literacy skills for a lifetime. Unlike riding a bicycle, which is a skill that once acquired is never forgotten, literacy must be maintained through regular and demanding practice.

Expanding the provision of adult education and training is another option open to policy-makers. But because of the voluntary nature that characterises much adult education, in this case the audience is likely to consist mostly of those who are motivated and enabled to learn, and who have access to the required resources. The survey data reported in Figure 3.4 overwhelmingly show that job-related adult education and training programmes tend to benefit the already well-educated, and that those most in need of literacy skills training are not always reached. While the degree of inequality in participation rates by initial education qualifications is larger in some countries (Germany, Switzerland, the United States) than in others (Australia, Finland, Sweden), the phenomenon itself is universal. Clearly, a strategy for improving the skills of low-literate adults will require action in addition to school improvement and the expansion of educational delivery for adults.

The data presented in the next sections examine the relationship between literacy proficiency and the uses made of literacy skills at work and in everyday life. The results would seem to indicate not only that regular practice appears to sustain and enhance performance in literacy, but also that workers in occupations and workplaces that demand and reward high literacy tend to have higher skill levels, given their educational attainment, than workers in firms where less of a premium is put on skill. This result, combined with the finding that high-literacy workplaces tend to be in high-wage and high-productivity sectors while low-literacy workplaces tend more often to be those in stagnation or decline

Figure 3.4
Participation in job-related adult education, by initial educational attainment
Participation rates (percentages) of employed persons aged 25-64 in job-related education and training over a 12-month period, selected countries, various years

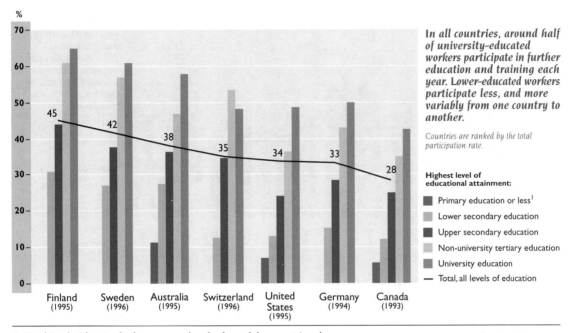

In all countries, around half of university-educated workers participate in further education and training each year. Lower-educated workers participate less, and more variably from one country to another.

Countries are ranked by the total participation rate.

Highest level of educational attainment:

■ Primary education or less[1]
■ Lower secondary education
■ Upper secondary education
■ Non-university tertiary education
■ University education
— Total, all levels of education

1. Combined with rates for lower secondary for four of the countries shown.
Source: OECD Education Database.

Data for Figure 3.4: page 107.

(see OECD and Statistics Canada, 1995), suggests that the key to addressing the literacy deficit in OECD countries lies in influencing workplace practice. This can only be achieved through a strategy based on partnerships for learning – one that makes the social partners, workers and the larger community not only aware of the benefits of high-literacy supporting environments, but also willing to shoulder more of the responsibility for skill development.

3.4 LITERACY PRACTICES AT WORK

A broad range of information about the respondents' literacy practices at work was collected as part of the survey. In general, there are differences among the countries in the frequencies reported for the uses of different literacy tasks at work, such as writing letters or memos, reading manuals, reports or articles, or dealing with diagrams, bills, invoices, or budget tables. There is a general tendency, across countries,

scales, and tasks, for individuals at higher literacy skill levels to report that they carry out a practice more frequently. The differences are larger for tasks that are likely to involve more complex texts, such as using manuals and reference books.

Australian, German, Swiss and Swedish employees tended to report the most frequent use of particular literacy tasks at work, and Irish and Polish workers the least frequent. These differences reflect the occupational distributions of the countries. Among the surveyed countries, Ireland and Poland have the largest proportion of workers in relatively low-skill occupations such as agriculture and primary industries. In general, Irish and Polish respondents not only tested more poorly compared to Germans or Swedes, but they also reported using relevant literacy skills the least often. At the same time, Poland recorded the smallest proportions in the occupations requiring the most frequent use of literacy skills: managers, technicians, and clerks.

Figure 3.5
Skilled craft workers' reading practices at work
Percentage who perform particular reading tasks at least once a week, 1994-1995

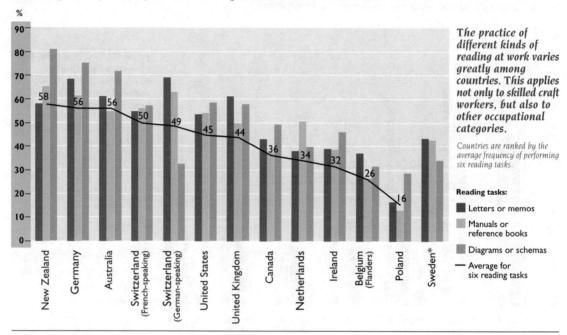

The practice of different kinds of reading at work varies greatly among countries. This applies not only to skilled craft workers, but also to other occupational categories.

Countries are ranked by the average frequency of performing six reading tasks.

Reading tasks:
- Letters or memos
- Manuals or reference books
- Diagrams or schemas
- Average for six reading tasks

* Did not ask all of the questions in comparable ways.

Source: OECD and Statistics Canada, International Adult Literacy Survey.

Data for Figure 3.5: page 107.

The frequency of reading tasks varies by occupation, as should be expected. Figure 3.5 shows as an example the variation between countries in reading practices at work for skilled craft workers.[4] In French-speaking Switzerland, the United Kingdom and the United States, for example, about 58 per cent of skilled craft workers said they read diagrams and schemas at work at least once a week. This compares to 72 per cent of Australian, 75 per cent of German, and 81 per cent of New Zealand craft workers, and between 29 and 34 per cent of Belgian (Flemish), Polish and Swedish workers. On an index based on six reading tasks, Australian, German, New Zealand and Swiss craft workers appear to read the most.

Overall, the occupational category with the highest reported frequencies of reading across all tasks is the professional and managerial group. Clerks and technicians consistently report the second most frequent use for many reading tasks. Between country differences are small for these occupational groups, but there is substantial variation across countries in the reading behaviours of less qualified

groups, such as plant and machine operators and workers in services and sales. Service workers in Belgium (Flanders), Germany, Sweden and Switzerland perform various reading tasks more frequently at work than similar workers in other countries.

Respondents were also asked how often they wrote or filled out four types of text as part of their job – letters or memos; forms or items such as bills, invoices, or budgets; reports or articles; and estimates or technical specifications. As was the case with the reading tasks, there are large differences among certain occupational groups in the frequency of writing at work. There are also significant between-country differences within the occupational groups.

Why do workers engage in literacy practices so much less in some kinds of job than in others? There are three potential explanations. First, that these practices are not needed, because they

4.   Note that the standard errors of the estimates are generally large.

Figure 3.6 **An untapped pool of talent**

a. Proportion of skilled craft workers and machine operators at literacy Levels 3 to 5, document scale, selected countries, 1994-1995

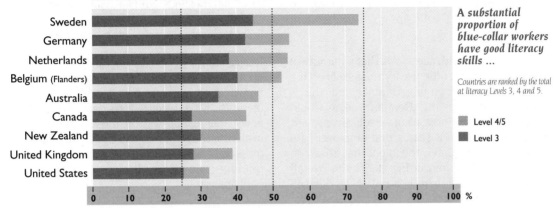

A *substantial proportion of blue-collar workers have good literacy skills ...*

Countries are ranked by the total at literacy Levels 3, 4 and 5.

■ Level 4/5
■ Level 3

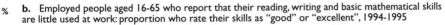

%   **b.** Employed people aged 16-65 who report that their reading, writing and basic mathematical skills are little used at work: proportion who rate their skills as "good" or "excellent", 1994-1995

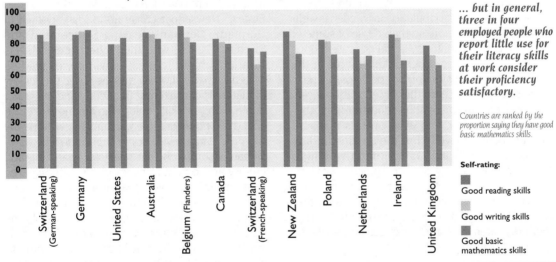

... but in general, three in four employed people who report little use for their literacy skills at work consider their proficiency satisfactory.

Countries are ranked by the proportion saying they have good basic mathematics skills.

Self-rating:

■ Good reading skills

Good writing skills

■ Good basic mathematics skills

Source: OECD and Statistics Canada, International Adult Literacy Survey.
Data for Figure 3.6: page 108.

simply do not relate to the demands of the job. Second, that they are needed but workers in certain occupations have low literacy skills and so employers are unable to set them challenging tasks. Third, that many workers do have the skills but they are insufficiently used.

The evidence indicates that while there is some element of truth in each of these three explanations, particular attention should be paid to the third one. While clearly the potential for using

different skills is bound to vary by occupation, the wide variations between countries shown in Figure 3.5 suggests that some work cultures find better ways of using skills than others. Such differences may go some way to explaining variations in productivity in different countries. The second explanation, that employers would like to use worker skills but they are constrained by the pool of talent, may be true in some cases but is not universally so. Figure 3.6 shows why not. A significant proportion of skilled blue-collar workers have medium to high literacy skills (Figure 3.6a). Yet among workers who report that they have little use for their literacy skills at work, the majority consider that their reading, writing and basic mathematics skills are good or excellent (Figure 3.6b).

The assessment evidence shows that a number of workers who report little use for their skills on the job overrate their own literacy ability, but this is not true for the majority. German workers would appear to have the most accurate self-assessment in this respect. So it seems that employers are failing to tap adequately the talent that exists. In the process, they are putting at risk the overall literacy pool, since there is a risk that skills will decline through lack of use.

This evidence could help to explain the results in the one country whose literacy performance stands clearly ahead of the others that have undertaken the survey. The adult population in Sweden is well-educated, but not more so than those of some of the comparison countries. Initial education does not explain all of the observed differences in the skill profiles across countries, perhaps, in part, because of differences in the way education levels are classified. Organised adult education is another contributing factor, and even on this measure Sweden performs well. But the striking finding is that Sweden also has comparatively high frequencies of reading and writing practices at work, not only by professionals, managers, technicians and clerks but also, and importantly, by many other categories of workers – crafts excepted. This "culture of literacy" in the workplace may explain a good part of literacy performance.

3.5 LITERACY AT HOME AND IN THE COMMUNITY

High literacy-supporting work environments are essential but attention needs to be given also to the uses of literacy in everyday life. The daily practice of reading, writing, and calculating must be assumed to sustain and enhance literacy skills, regardless of whether the practice occurs at work or in another setting. The survey collected data about literacy practices at home and in the community, and compared these with the workplace. For the majority of countries a consistent finding is that, for most literacy practices, the workplace provides a richer environment than the home or the community in terms of offering opportunities for reading. Although this finding underscores the importance of the workplace in literacy development, much literacy activity also takes place elsewhere.

Respondents were asked a variety of questions about their everyday literacy practices and their participation in community organisations. Of all literacy activities practised on a daily or weekly basis, newspaper reading was the most common activity in all countries studied. The overall frequencies for three activities are shown in Figure 3.7: newspaper reading, television viewing, and community participation.

Daily newspaper reading is fairly common in all of the surveyed countries, although less so in countries with large numbers of second-language speakers, as in Belgium (Flanders), Canada and the United States. Newspaper consumption is very high in Germany, German-speaking Switzerland and Sweden. People with the highest literacy skills invariably had the greatest variety of reading materials in their homes, and they used this variety of materials consistently, frequently and in greater depth than low-skill adults, who are more likely to spend two hours or more watching television every day. The data provide some support for the wide-spread assumption that television watching and literacy are somehow incompatible, although the relationship is complex. There is a noticeable – and negative – link between the two: those most likely to watch television for significant periods of time are usually at lower literacy levels. Low skills possibly lead to more viewing time because those with low skills may not be able to get the information they need from print, and turn to television instead (ETS, 1996). Figure 3.7 also points to considerable differences in community participation across countries, with one-third or more of the population in Sweden and the United States engaging in voluntary community activities, compared with between one-fifth and one-quarter in most of the countries surveyed.

3.6 THE ROLE OF EMPLOYERS IN LITERACY

For all concerned by the problem of how to raise the literacy levels of low-skilled adults, the finding that the workplace affords more frequent

Figure 3.7
Newspaper reading, television viewing and community participation
Proportion of population aged 16-65 who reported engaging in each of the three activities, 1994-1995

There are wide variations in how many people in different countries practice habits associated with high or low literacy...

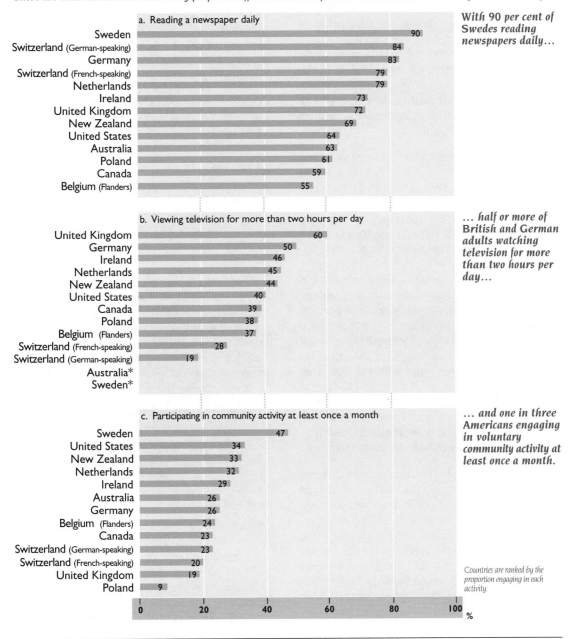

With 90 per cent of Swedes reading newspapers daily...

... half or more of British and German adults watching television for more than two hours per day...

... and one in three Americans engaging in voluntary community activity at least once a month.

Countries are ranked by the proportion engaging in each activity.

* Did not ask question.
Source: OECD and Statistics Canada, International Adult Literacy Survey.
Data for Figure 3.7: page 108.

opportunities to practice literacy skills than the home may provide a possible answer to the policy dilemma posed. This gives employers a larger role to play in the development and maintenance of literacy skills than previously assumed.

Private firms and public employers already play an important role in creating incentives in favour of adult literacy through compensation structures that nearly universally reward more learning better than less learning. This can be observed in the returns to formal education as well as literacy proficiency. Box 3B mentions some of the anticipated returns to employers who invest in literacy skill development.

The workplace may well provide the answer, and the benefits seem to be clear, but how might enterprises best go about raising and reinforcing adult literacy? Despite the ample indications as to the expected benefits, firms vary in the extent to which they attach importance to workplace literacy. These differences are apparent in the qualifications firms seek when they hire individuals, and in the human resource development practices they pursue in further developing those qualifications and thus sustaining high levels of literacy. Though firms vary with respect to the importance attached to workplace literacy, there is a growing body of evidence that suggests that profitability depends increasingly on the ability of an enterprise to adapt without delay to changes in market conditions, and to exploit rapidly business opportunities as they arise. Moreover, the knowledge and skills of workers are important determinants of the capacity of firms to adapt quickly.

The emphasis on raising and reinforcing workforce literacy is typically associated with a number of other forms of innovations in business strategy, internal work organisation, and external relations with suppliers, customers, and other firms. Thus, enterprises that place a premium on the literacy levels of their workers tend to be the same ones that train more and whose workforces are relatively highly qualified. The implications vary from employer to employer. Two broad practices characterise the firms that explicitly pursue strategies of raising and reinforcing workplace literacy: incentives and the enabling mechanisms they adopt to encourage learning. Examples of such practices are examined below.

Box 3B
BENEFITS FROM ENHANCED LITERACY IN THE WORKPLACE

A study conducted by the Conference Board of Canada (1997) concludes that there are a number of clear economic benefits in improving workplace literacy, but the message has not yet reached many employers:

• *Increased ability to handle training on the job and quicker training results* – Literacy training strengthens employees' ability to work with oral and written material and to grasp new concepts.

• *Better team performance* -- Successful teamwork requires understanding and communication: stronger literacy skills provide both; employees with improved literacy skills learn about and understand areas of the organisation other than their own and are more willing to participate in dialogue.

• *Improved labour-management relations* – Enhanced literacy skills support the objectives of both labour and management: workers value the courses and view their existence as a positive signal that management is prepared to invest in them, and the employers value education and a learning culture within the organisation. Turnover and absenteeism might be reduced as a result.

• *Increased quality* – Employees with improved literacy skills make fewer errors and have greater confidence in their ability to communicate. They are also more engaged and participative at work and put their knowledge to better use, providing valuable feedback affecting product quality and productivity.

• *Reduced time per task and improved efficiency* – Enhanced literacy skills reduce the time needed to process written information, such as manuals, and to complete paperwork. Higher literacy levels can help ensure that the organisation is moving in the same direction: this alignment can make an important contribution to increasing efficiency and profitability.

Source: Adapted from the Conference Board of Canada (1997).

Compensation is a key incentive. As indicated above, rates of return to formal education and relative earnings of individuals according to their qualifications indicate the value that firms attach to *initial* educational qualifications (see Chapter 2). Wage-tenure profiles provide some indication of the extent to which work experience – which could further enhance literacy – is rewarded. Large Japanese firms offer useful lessons on the importance of compensation systems for encouraging literacy. The Japanese labour force is well-qualified in terms of having few persons with low qualification levels. It also compares well with other countries with respect to the proportion of workers who participate in workplace training, and with respect to the evident flexibility that enterprises have in adopting innovations in the workplace. Japanese firms rely heavily on compensation schemes to create incentives for participation in various forms of work-based training. These schemes do this by rewarding both learning and teaching. Wages are based in substantial part on the breadth and depth of worker skills. Breadth is evaluated by supervisors in terms of the number of different tasks individuals can perform; depth is evaluated in terms of the level of proficiency: the lowest being whether an individual can perform a task under supervision, the highest being whether an individual can teach the task to others. This incentive structure is reinforced through standard and transparent practices for assessing what it is that individuals know. Such assessment is based on reviews of their performance in carrying out different tasks, in different jobs, under different supervisors (Genda, 1996; see also Dore *et al.*, 1989). Faced with such an award structure, workers have clear incentives to continue learning during their employment, and to ensure that they pass along their own skills and know-how to others.

However, rewarding learning in a relatively structured context is not enough. A high-literacy supportive environment depends also on there being strong incentives for individuals to take the initiative in innovating, and to apply their skills in order to find ways to improve performance. In this regard, "suggestion boxes" or similar devices can encourage flows of innovative thinking outside the usual hierarchical structure that govern information flows. As such, they can serve as a means of reinforcing workplace literacy.

In addition to providing pay-related incentives, firms encourage literacy through the decisions affecting the contexts of workplace learning, and the forms learning can subsequently take. With respect to the decision context, there is evidence to indicate that flexible enterprises treat human resource development decisions strategically, as a part of more comprehensive changes in business strategy, technology, and organisation. This can be seen in findings from selected countries:

- In *Sweden*, firms that are moving towards more flexible forms of work organisation are two-thirds more likely than others to draw up plans for individual competence development. Furthermore, such competence development is more likely to be carried out close to the workplace, rather than in formal settings. Thus, although they are only about a tenth more likely to offer formal education, they are nearly three times more likely to make competence development part of daily work (NUTEK, 1996).

- Manufacturing enterprises in *France* also show high correlation between changes in tasks and the provision of training. Moreover, the correlation between a change in qualification requirements and the provision of training in flexible enterprises is sufficiently similar at different skill levels (0.40 for production workers, 0.41 for technicians and skilled workers, and 0.44 for engineers and professionals) to suggest that such firms are not likely to show the wide disparities in participation in training by qualification level that is commonly observed in French firms overall (Greenan, 1995, p. 11).

- In the *United States* there is evidence of fairly consistent, though less marked differences in the training behaviours of firms that reorganise and those that do not. The differences are clearest among establishments with fewer than 50 employees. Those that introduce work teams, total quality management, peer review of employee performance, pay for knowledge, or employee involvement in decisions on acquisition of technology and equipment are roughly a quarter more likely to provide skill training than those that do not. Similar relationships are found in medium and large establishments, although the differences between those that innovate and those that do not are smaller (Frazis et al., 1995, p. 16). Another study of training practices in US firms found that the use of benchmarking practices to improve enterprise performance and organisational changes, such as the introduction of total quality management, were associated with a higher propensity to train, particularly in manufacturing, other factors being equal (Lynch and Black, 1995, p. 11).

• In Canada the introduction of new technologies, strongly associated with the decision to train (Johnson et al., 1995, pp. 40-42), is also associated with strategic use of training. A Canadian survey of technology use found that more than two-thirds of firms introducing computer-based technology in the period 1986-91 sponsored skills training to meet the new qualification requirements. Furthermore, throughout the 1980s, decisions about who would receive training were a function of the diffusion and use of computer-based technologies rather than of larger developments such as organisational change (Betcherman et al., 1994, p. 38).

In addition to the changing patterns of training associated with the reorganisation of firms, changes are also observed in the means of providing training and, more broadly, in the way in which learning occurs. There are particularly important changes with respect to the application of formal and informal learning methods and the use of specific employee development strategies. Evidence suggests that it is particularly important to build on what individuals already know, to situate learning "in context", and to relate it to what occurs on the

job (OECD, 1996). In this regard, Japanese firms have been successful in achieving high levels of participation in workplace training among all workers, even relatively poorly qualified ones.

There is little evidence on the long-term cost-effectiveness of adult literacy programmes aimed at poorly qualified adults. It would appear that, at a minimum, such programmes need to incorporate a number of features, including open entry/open exit, individualised and self-pace learning, multiple-strand curriculum, flexible hours, and flexible locations. An evaluation of workplace literacy programmes in Canada and the United States indicates that for such programmes to be effective, they need to be based on an analysis of the skills needed for specific jobs, be well-integrated with work-based technical training, and be accompanied by counselling and linkage to on-the-job training. To be effective, such programmes are likely to be resource intensive, requiring 50-100 hours of instruction for each year of gain (Mikulecky, 1995).

How much of a role can enterprises be expected to play in providing literacy training for their poorly qualified workers? The current situation is not encouraging. Those enterprises that follow practices that reinforce literacy and encourage further learning are, on average, the same ones that hire and retain adults who are already more qualified. In terms of overall training patterns poorly qualified adults are at a disadvantage, in part because they are less likely to be employed in flexible enterprises, or because they lack the prerequisite qualifications for specific training. The particular learning needs of poorly qualified adults are therefore seldom met fully through firm-based training. If programmatic practices over the last decade are any indication, the prospects for adequate basic literacy training to be provided by employers seem bleak. Even if employers who understand the benefits of literacy were to assume more responsibility for provision, there will therefore remain a large demand for public intervention programmes in literacy. But the responsibility for creating a high literacy supporting environment is shared not only by employers and communities. Ultimately it is the individual who has a large role to play.

3.7 CONCLUSIONS

Overall, it would appear that enterprises are moving in the direction of favouring higher literacy levels and more work-based learning. But this trend favours workers with higher initial levels of literacy and qualifications. This would suggest that, without some marked shift in enterprise employment and training practices, enterprises are not likely to meet fully the needs of the least qualified adults for basic literacy training. Moreover, changes in work-based learning need to be accompanied by more active use of literacy skills at work, particularly in occupations below the managerial and professional levels.

Increasingly, those with fewer and low-level skills are finding that they are being excluded from a job market which offers employment only to the highly skilled. The gap between "low skilled" and "high skilled" has significant implications for social cohesion in all OECD countries. For individuals, the consequences of poor literacy skills are fewer job opportunities and limited earning capacity; for nations, the lack of a highly skilled workforce can mean an inability to take advantage of the opportunities offered by the new global marketplace. ∎

References

BETCHERMAN, G.K., McMULLEN, K., LECHIE, N. and **CARON, C.** (1994), *The Canadian Workplace in Transition*, Industrial Relations Centre, Queen's University, Kingston, Ontario.

CONFERENCE BOARD OF CANADA (1997), *The Economic Benefits of Improving Literacy Skills in the Workplace*, The Conference Board of Canada, Ottawa, Ontario.

DORE, R., BOUNINE-CABALÉ, J. and **TAPIOLA, K.** (1989), *Japan at Work: Markets, Management and Flexibility*, OECD, Paris.

ETS (Educational Testing Service) (1996), "Literacy: Economic key for the new millennium", ETS *Policy Notes*, Vol. 7, No. 1.

FRAZIS, H.J., HERZ, D.E. and **HORRIGAN, M.W.** (1995), "Employer-provided training: Results from a new survey", *Monthly Labor Review*, Vol. 118 (5), pp. 3-17.

GENDA, Y. (1996), "Changes in compensation systems in Japan", Paper prepared for the International Conference on Changing Workplace Strategies: Achieving Better Outcomes for Enterprises, Workers and Society, Ottawa, Ontario, 2-3 December.

GREENAN, N. (1995), "Technologie, changement organisationnel, qualifications et emploi: Une étude empirique sur l'industrie manufacturière", *Document de travail G9504*, INSEE, Paris, April.

JOHNSON, J., BALDWIN, J.R. and **DIVERTY, B.** (1995), "The implications of innovation and technological change for employment and human resource strategy", Mimeo, OECD, Paris, March.

KIRSCH, I.S., JENKINS, L., JUNGEBLUT, A. and **KOLSTAD, A.** (1993), *Adult Literacy in America: A First Look at the Results of the National Adult Literacy Survey*, National Center for Education Statistics, United States Department of Education, Washington, D.C.

LYNCH, L.M. and **BLACK, S.E.** (1995), "Beyond the incidence of training: Evidence from a national employers survey", NBER *Working Paper No. 5231*, National Bureau for Economic Research, Cambridge, Massachusetts.

MIKULECKY, L. (1994), "Workplace literacy programs: Organisation and incentives", in D. Hirsch and D.A. Wagner (eds.), *What Makes Workers Learn: The Role of Incentives in Workplace Education and Training*, Hampton Press, Cresskil, New Jersey.

MONTIGNY, G., KELLY, K. and **JONES, S.** (1991), *Adult Literacy in Canada: Results of a National Study*, Minister of Industry, Science and Technology, Ottawa, Ontario.
......

MURRAY, T.S., KIRSCH, I.S. and **JENKINS, L.** (eds.) (1997), *Adult Literacy in OECD Countries: Technical Report on the International Adult Literacy Survey*, National Center for Education Statistics, United States Department of Education, Washington, D.C.

NUTEK (1996), *Towards Flexible Organisations*, NUTEK Analys, Stockholm.

OECD (1992), *Adult Illiteracy and Economic Performance*, Paris.

OECD (1996), *Lifelong Learning for All*, Paris.

OECD and **STATISTICS CANADA** (1995), *Literacy, Economy and Society: Results of the First International Adult Literacy Survey*, Paris and Ottawa.

OECD and **STATISTICS CANADA** (1997), *Literacy Skills for the Knowledge Society: Further Results from the International Adult Literacy Survey*, Paris and Ottawa.

TUIJNMAN, A.C., KIRSCH, I.S. and **WAGNER, D.A.** (eds.) (1997), *Adult Basic Skills: Advances in Measurement and Policy Analysis*, Hampton Press, Cresskil, New Jersey.

WICKERT, R. (1989), *No Single Measure: A Survey of Australian Adult Literacy*, The Commonwealth Department of Employment, Education and Training, Canberra.

CHAPTER 4

FAILURE AT SCHOOL: PATTERNS AND RESPONSES

SUMMARY

There is a strong perception of a problem of "failure" in OECD education systems in terms of preparing all young people adequately for the demanding challenges of today's societies. This chapter presents evidence on several dimensions of low achievement, drawing on a recent study on "failure at school" (OECD, 1996a), which confirms that there is significant under-achievement by students in certain Member countries. The evidence shows that:

- Countries with poor average performance are also more likely to have a high proportion of low-achieving students;
- There is a wide gap between the highest and lowest achievers of the same age within each country, with an achievement range equivalent to up to four years of schooling; and
- Student achievement does not have to be widely dispersed in order for a system to perform well overall.

The data show that social background and in some respects also gender continue to be associated with disparities in student achievement. They also confirm that the greatest risks of marginalisation, unemployment or low income are no longer confined to early school leavers, but include a significant proportion of young people with upper secondary qualifications and above, whose reading and numeracy skills are low.

Overcoming educational failure requires a sustained and long-term effort to meet the needs of all students by improving schools, programmes and systems in each specific national context. Despite the variety of measures involved, some general policy principles include:

- The need to confront rather than ignore "failure". Policy-makers need to review their education systems and identify the extent and form of under-achievement by students, which can have damaging social and economic costs.
- The need to look at the system as a whole, and identify where targeted intervention is likely to have knock-on benefits. A consensus is developing on the value of pre-school education as laying a crucial foundation for future learning.
- The importance of clear leadership to mobilise public opinion around a strategy to combat failure and to ensure that all agencies are working in the same direction.
- The doubtful value of grade repetition and the need to look for more flexible ways of assisting students who fall behind at school, especially by individualising instruction and aid, and by assessing student strengths and weaknesses accurately.
- The importance of strategies to combat drop-out, recognising that its causes are complex. A more flexible curriculum, smoother pathways and transitions across levels, and improved educational and career guidance are three key measures that can help in combating the problem.
- The need for qualifications that accurately certify skills that will be useful on the labour market, in light of the significant number of graduates from secondary education who at present apparently lack a minimum level of performance in certain foundation skills.
- The need for better statistics and indicators that can inform the comparative knowledge base on educational success and failure.

4.1 INTRODUCTION

In many OECD countries there is widespread concern about the increasingly damaging consequences of under-achievement and low attainment. Educational failure has become:

- punitive for the individual, in terms of unemployment or low earnings;
- harmful for society as a whole, in terms of reduced economic competitiveness and social cohesion; and
- a heavy burden for educational systems, in terms of wasted resources at a time of restraint in government spending.

Despite measures that educational authorities have undertaken to overcome system, school and student failure, the problem persists in all OECD countries, although in different forms and to varying degrees. This chapter looks at dimensions of low achievement by students and at how it can be overcome. It proposes ways to identify it, examines the main contributing factors, and discusses what under-achievement can mean for the productive integration of young people into modern society. Finally, it points to key issues for developing better policies.

4.2 HOW TO IDENTIFY AND ADDRESS LOW ACHIEVEMENT

In all OECD countries, some students have difficulty in following the programmes of study set out in the curriculum. This is reflected in the fact that there is a significant diversity of performance among pupils of the same age or year group. Despite the manifold differences between national education systems, various international studies – notably those conducted by the International Association for the Evaluation of Educational Achievement (IEA) – show that it is possible to develop comparative measures of some aspects of student achievement, by assessing the performance of similar samples of students from each participating country on a common test. Such data[1] can be used to determine:

- which pupils can be seen as low-achievers in relation to an *international* average; and
- which pupils can, on a *national* basis, be considered most at risk of failing at school.

Low achievement compared to an international standard

Figure 4.1 presents, for each OECD country that participated in the IEA studies of reading literacy, mathematics and science achievement, the proportion of pupils aged around 13-14 years whose test scores are substantially below the average score for all the OECD countries that took part in the study. Under-achievement in this case is defined as scoring at least one standard deviation below the international mean, a statistical description that covers roughly the lowest-scoring 15 per cent of children across countries. The students scoring lowest on these tests can therefore be considered as "low-achievers", in spite of the considerable differences in curricula among countries.

In some countries, the proportion of "weak" pupils is substantially lower than the expected 15 per cent:

- for *reading*, it is below 11 per cent in France, Portugal, Sweden and Switzerland, and below 5 per cent in Finland;
- for *mathematics*, it is below 10 per cent in Belgium (Flemish Community), the Czech Republic, France, Korea and Switzerland, and below 5 per cent in Japan;
- for *science*, it is below 10 per cent in Austria, Belgium (Flemish Community), Hungary, Japan, Korea and the Netherlands, and below 5 per cent in the Czech Republic.

At the other end of the scale, some countries have a markedly higher proportion of school children with low achievement:

- in *reading*, for which the proportion of low achievers is over 20 per cent in Ireland and Spain, and almost 30 per cent in Belgium (French Community);
- in *mathematics*, for which over 20 per cent of children in England, Greece, Iceland,

---

1.   The 1990-91 IEA Reading Literacy Study of 14-year-olds (applied in 32 countries, 19 of which are OECD Members) and the 1994-95 Third International Mathematics and Science Study (TIMSS) of "13 year-olds" (applied in 45 countries, 23 of which are from the OECD area). The target population studied by TIMSS is the upper grade of the two grade levels in which most 13-year-olds are enrolled and which, by convention, is referred to as the "8th grade" since in most countries it refers to the eighth year of formal schooling. See Elley (1992); Beaton *et al.* (1996); Martin *et al.* (1997); and Mullis *et al.* (1997).

Figure 4.1
Low achievement compared to an international standard
Percentage of students scoring below standard

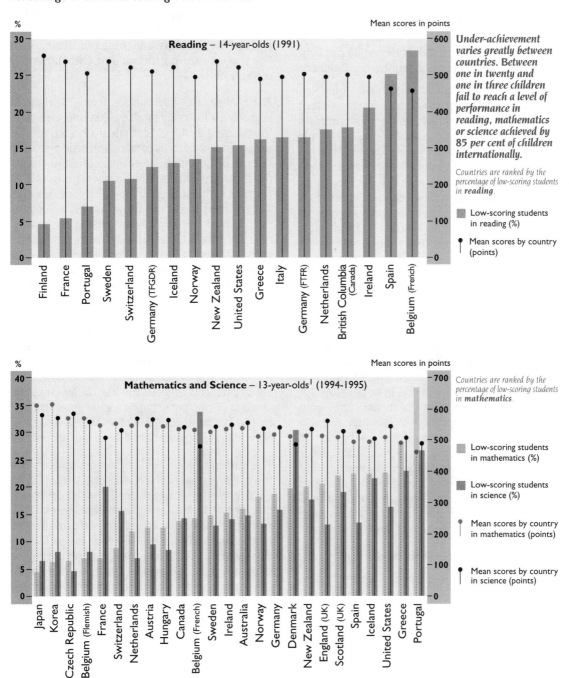

Under-achievement varies greatly between countries. Between one in twenty and one in three children fail to reach a level of performance in reading, mathematics or science achieved by 85 per cent of children internationally.

Countries are ranked by the percentage of low-scoring students in **reading**.

▓ Low-scoring students in reading (%)

● Mean scores by country (points)

Countries are ranked by the percentage of low-scoring students in **mathematics**.

▓ Low-scoring students in mathematics (%)

▓ Low-scoring students in science (%)

● Mean scores by country in mathematics (points)

● Mean scores by country in science (points)

1. "8th grade" students; "7th grade" for students in Denmark.
Sources: IEA, *Reading Literacy Study*; IEA, *Third International Mathematics and Science Study*.
Data and notes for Figure 4.1: page 109.

New Zealand, Spain and the United States, and nearly 40 per cent in Portugal, perform poorly; or

• in *science*, for which over 20 per cent of students under-achieve in France, Greece, Iceland and Portugal, and over 30 per cent in Belgium (French Community) and Denmark.

Since fewer than half of the OECD countries participated in the three studies, no consistent pattern of under-achievement across subjects can be identified for the OECD area. The only countries showing a fairly consistent profile are Sweden, where in none of the subjects do more than 15 per cent of children under-achieve, and the United States and New Zealand, where in all three subjects the proportion with low scores exceeds 15 per cent. The best example of a country with mixed results is France, where only 5 per cent of children under-achieve in reading, and 7 per cent in mathematics, compared with 20 per cent in science.

The evidence shows a clear relationship between the percentage of "low-achievers" and the mean scores attained in reading, mathematics and science by the entire student population. This need not be the case: in a country with an unequal distribution of achievement it is possible for higher-achievers to raise the mean score, even though a large proportion of children are also under-achieving. This appears to be the case in New Zealand for reading: its average score places it amongst the higher-performing countries, but it still has 15 per cent of "weak" readers. But this case is atypical: most countries with above-average mean scores also have a below-average proportion of weak performers, and vice versa.

The range of achievement within countries

Another way of identifying under-achievement is to examine, within each country, the divergence in performance between the lowest and the highest scoring students on a given test. If this divergence in achievement is found to be equivalent to several years of schooling, then the poor performing students are at a great risk of failing at school or dropping out.

As can be seen from Figure 4.2, in all OECD countries that participated in the IEA Reading

Literacy and TIMSS studies, there is a significant gap between the scores attained by the lowest and the highest scoring students. A standardised measure of this gap looks in each country at the score below which the bottom quarter of the population performs, and the score above which the top quarter performs, and calculates the difference.[2]

For *reading*, the gap ranges from 73 points in Portugal to 136 points in New Zealand (see data for Figure 4.2 in the Statistical Annex). These ranges in point scores carry no intrinsic meaning, but can be better understood by looking at how much progress is made on average in OECD countries by a student in one year (see Box 4A). The results for reading show that in each country the best scoring 14-year-olds in the bottom quarter of the population is 2-4 years behind the worst-scoring 14-year-olds in the top quarter – a wide range of achievement by any standard. Similar patterns can be observed for performance in mathematics and science. The difference in achievement between the lowest and highest scoring students is equivalent to between 2 and 3 years of schooling for *science*; and it even reaches 4 years in some countries for *mathematics*. So in all school systems in all three subjects there is a substantial gap between the level attained by the weakest 25 per cent of pupils and the level attained by the strongest 25 per cent in the same grade, equivalent to between 2 and 4 years of schooling.[3]

The difference in achievement between the lowest and the highest scoring students, in each country, appears to be wider in those countries that attain higher mean scores. This is particularly the case for performance in mathematics. There are, however, exceptions to this pattern. The widest range of achievement in reading is found in New Zealand while one of the narrowest is found in Finland; both countries with high average reading scores. On the other

---

2. This "inter-quartile range" is the difference between the 25th percentile and the 75th percentile, a measure commonly used to study the range of performance. It also represents the range of scores achieved by the "middle" 50 per cent of the population.

3. The smaller difference in achievement observed for Portugal, across all three subjects, might be due partly to the number of children in that country who dropped out of school or repeated a year of study before the testing age.

Figure 4.2
Range of achievement within countries
Lower and upper quartiles, relative to international mean, in equivalent years' progress

Difference between lower or upper quartile
and the international mean (including non-OECD countries) in equivalent years' progress

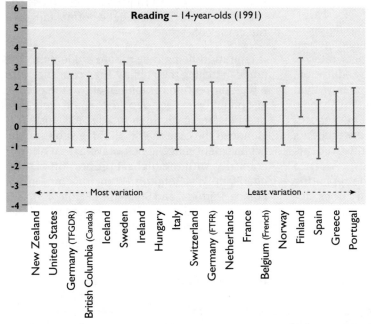

For reading, the range of achievement in the middle scoring 50 per cent of children equates to between 2 1/2 and 4 1/2 years' progress.

Countries are ranked by the variation in reading achievement.

⊤ Upper quartile
⊥ Lower quartile

Difference between lower or upper quartile and the OECD mean in equivalent years' progress

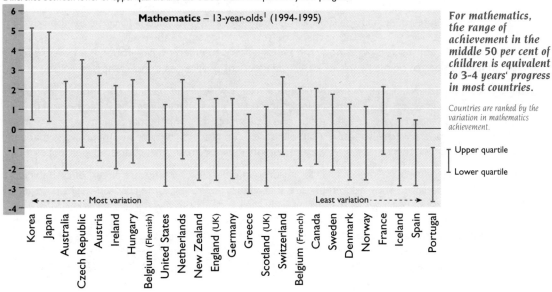

For mathematics, the range of achievement in the middle 50 per cent of children is equivalent to 3-4 years' progress in most countries.

Countries are ranked by the variation in mathematics achievement.

⊤ Upper quartile
⊥ Lower quartile

---

1. "8th grade" students; "7th grade" for students in Denmark.
Sources: IEA, *Reading Literacy Study*; IEA, *Third International Mathematics and Science Study*.
Data and notes for Figure 4.2: pages 110-111.

hand, a moderate range of achievement in science can be found in Belgium (Flemish Community) and the Netherlands; both countries with high average scores in science. These exceptions show that *a wide range of achievement is not a necessary condition for a system to attain a high average level of performance*.

Certain OECD countries respond to differences in achievement by making some children repeat grades. Countries tend to have higher rates of repetition in secondary than primary education, and repetition rates that are higher for boys than for girls (OECD, 1996a, pp. 25-26). Although there are seemingly strong arguments for making students repeat grades (granting slower students more time to learn and protecting other students from being delayed in their studies), evidence from many investigations of grade repeating shows that this approach not only does not reduce but actually *increases the problem of under-*

achievement. In some of the countries where grade-repeating exists, one finds a substantial proportion of students who – due to the effects of repetition in their schooling process – are over-aged for the grade they are enrolled in. Figure 4.3 shows the proportion of students, in the IEA Reading Literacy and TIMSS samples, whose age could be considered above the normal range for the grade concerned.

If repetition helps redistribute students to the grade matching their ability, then countries with a high proportion of children above the normal age might be expected to have a narrower range of achievement within the grade being tested. It is indeed the case that in all three subjects, the achievement range is below average in all four countries with the highest proportion of over-aged pupils – Belgium (French Community), France, Portugal and Spain (see Figure 4.3). But the data also show that the students of "above

---

Box 4A
CHILDREN'S PROGRESS MEASURED IN YEARS: HANDLE WITH CARE

When comparing the achievement of children in different countries, there is no obvious yardstick against which to measure their progress. Each country has its own way of measuring progress against the requirements of the curriculum. International tests run by the IEA construct an artificial scale, assigning a point score to each child. One way of understanding this scale is to compare the point score of children at different ages sitting the same test, or to compare their scores on certain common items in different tests. By looking at the average score of different age-groups, it is possible to calculate the number of points by which an average student progresses in one year.

The IEA tested both 9- and 14-year-old children in reading. On the basis of common items, the average difference in score was 155 points for children five years apart in age. So it can be said that 31 points corresponds, on average, to about one year's progress. Mathematics and science tests taken by eighth graders were also sat by a sample of seventh graders, to measure the progress made in a year. The younger children's scores were 33 points lower in mathematics and 40 in science.

These measures give a rough idea of how far children in different countries are ahead of or behind the international average. They also emphasise that within countries, some children might have to work for several years just to get to the level already achieved by others within their grade. But such comparisons have their limits. Comparing the achievement of children in different grades with different curricula is not the same as comparing differences between children within the same grade. So saying, for example, that some countries' eighth-graders are "more than three years ahead" of others in mathematics, means only that the difference in the countries' average eighth-grade scores is over three times the difference between seventh and eighth graders across OECD countries. It cannot be inferred that eighth-graders in some countries are tackling the problems being set to 11th-graders in others. Doing well on the curriculum for your own grade does not mean that you have already learned the curriculum for higher ones.

Figure 4.3
Handicap of over-aged students
Difference from national mean, on index from -1(most behind) to +1 (most ahead)

■ Mathematics handicap (1994-1995)
■ Reading handicap (1991)

Percentage of over-aged students

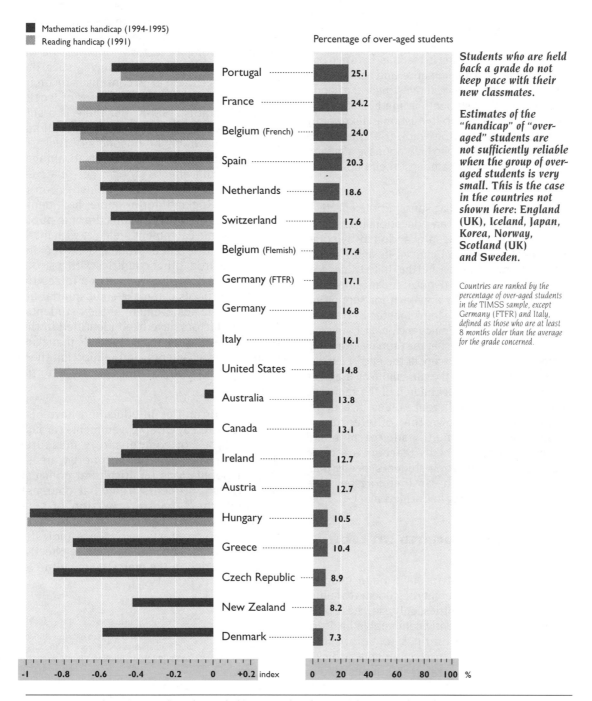

Students who are held back a grade do not keep pace with their new classmates.

Estimates of the "handicap" of "over-aged" students are not sufficiently reliable when the group of over-aged students is very small. This is the case in the countries not shown here: England (UK), Iceland, Japan, Korea, Norway, Scotland (UK) and Sweden.

Countries are ranked by the percentage of over-aged students in the TIMSS sample, except Germany (FTFR) and Italy, defined as those who are at least 8 months older than the average for the grade concerned.

Country	%
Portugal	25.1
France	24.2
Belgium (French)	24.0
Spain	20.3
Netherlands	18.6
Switzerland	17.6
Belgium (Flemish)	17.4
Germany (FTFR)	17.1
Germany	16.8
Italy	16.1
United States	14.8
Australia	13.8
Canada	13.1
Ireland	12.7
Austria	12.7
Hungary	10.5
Greece	10.4
Czech Republic	8.9
New Zealand	8.2
Denmark	7.3

Sources: IEA, *Reading Literacy Study*, and IEA, *Third International Mathematics and Science Study.*
Data and notes for Figure 4.3: page 112.

normal" age have more trouble in reading, mathematics and science than their classmates, which suggests that repetition is not doing much to improve the skills of the pupils held back for a year or more. In most countries, the gap between their average ability and that of "normal age" pupils is the equivalent of between two and three years worth of schooling in reading; between one and three years in mathematics, and between one and two years in science. Interestingly, the handicap of over-aged students in mathematics and science is close to zero in Australia. Also worthy of note is the fact that the Nordic countries, where repetition is not practised, do not have a greater range of achievement amongst their pupils than other countries.

The serious doubts that surround the effectiveness of repetition as an educational approach explain why it has been abandoned by some countries (for example, Denmark, Ireland, Finland, Greece, Norway, Sweden and the United Kingdom) or restricted by others (France, and most recently Portugal). A different approach for supporting "slow learners" is being implemented by Belgium (French Community), France and Spain, by moving into a system of "cycles" at the primary level, with repetition forbidden except at the end of a cycle. The aim is to structure the curriculum on the basis of longer units, so that children of the same age group may be in different stages of a cycle. Experience has shown that differentiated, individualised and multi-grade teaching and formative assessment by teachers are more flexible ways of meeting students' needs than grade repetition, and can therefore be more effective in addressing low achievement.

4.3 FACTORS ASSOCIATED WITH LOW ACHIEVEMENT

Although many factors have been used to account for the vulnerability of students to failure in various OECD countries, only a few have been surveyed on a sufficiently comparable basis for an analysis of the findings to be possible internationally. Evidence on student achievement in the OECD area[4] makes it possible to comment on three such factors: low socio-economic background, gender and membership of a linguistic minority.

Social differences persist

Social differences continue to be an important source of disparities in student achievement, notwithstanding the considerable efforts undertaken by OECD education systems to guarantee "equal opportunities for all". It is problematic to compare across countries the degree of progress made in reducing such disparities, since there is no consensus on an internationally comparable indicator of "socio-economic status" (SES). But there is a substantial body of evidence showing that children must not inevitably be prisoners of their social background: schools with disadvantaged intakes, if run effectively, can get relatively good results. The systematic inspection of schools in England, for example, has identified neighbouring institutions drawing pupils from the same catchment area, yet with markedly different levels of student achievement. Experience from other countries with a strong focus on school improvement reinforces the view that schools can make a substantial difference in the achievement of their students.[5] Two main factors have been identified in this respect: developing teachers' skills in making formative assessments, and reinforcing these assessments through some form of external evaluation.

Equal opportunities in education have also been promoted by OECD governments through various types of compensatory measures directed at specific schools (priority areas), student populations (multicultural policies), or individual students (remedial courses). Although the separate provision of such special education programmes might be called for in certain contexts, experience indicates that they could "become much more effective once embedded in the mainstream culture of the system" (OECD, 1997).

---

4. Background characteristics of the 15 per cent of those students scoring lowest in reading, mathematics and science, in the OECD countries which participated in the IEA Reading Literacy Study and TIMSS.

5. School improvement has become the main policy focus of measures addressing failure in Australia, New Zealand and the United Kingdom. Some US states and Canadian provinces have also embraced this approach.

Gender differences continue for the weakest

In most countries, there are more boys than girls in the group of pupils with the lowest reading scores, but the reverse is true of performance in mathematics and science. In terms of overall achievement in reading and mathematics, there are few statistically significant differences between boys and girls for the majority of countries (Elley, 1992; Beaton *et al.*, 1996; Mullis *et al.*, 1997). Fourth-grade boys do better than girls in mathematics in Japan, Korea and the Netherlands, and they have significantly higher mean science achievement than girls in Australia, Austria, Czech Republic, Iceland, Japan, Korea, the Netherlands, and the United States. Significant differences in mean achievement favouring boys range from 12 points in the United States to 26 points in the Netherlands (Martin *et al.*, 1997, p. 33). With respect to mathematics achievement, significant gender differences are found in Denmark and Korea (Beaton *et al.*, 1996). Although a tendency has been observed over the past few decades for gender differences to become less marked, major differences remain at the lower end of the achievement scale.[6] Clearly, a greater effort needs to be made to reduce such differences.

Linguistic minorities tend to be less disadvantaged in some countries than in others

Many education systems are confronted with the specific problem of how to integrate students coming from immigrant backgrounds, whose mother tongues are different from the language of instruction. The linguistic handicap experienced by these pupils is often compounded by a second, socio-economic handicap.[7] The size, ethnic origin, and social status of these minorities differ from one country to the other, so comparisons are difficult to make. However, the evidence reflects a trend that warrants more detailed analysis: *in some education systems, there seems to be less risk than in others of poor reading skills being associated with membership of a linguistic minority* (see OECD, 1995, 1996a). Yet the special programmes set up to facilitate the integration of minority pupils have been shown in studies to be effective only in some cases, once the data

are corrected for different characteristics of the immigrant population across countries. Such comparisons will become more important as international migration increases. This trend warrants an effort to gather better data, at the national and international levels.

4.4 ECONOMIC AND SOCIAL VULNERABILITY OF LOW-ACHIEVING STUDENTS

The evidence on youth employment during the last decade shows that young people with inadequate skills and competencies face a growing threat of low income or complete economic marginalisation (OECD, 1994). Educational authorities in OECD countries have therefore focused on two important manifestations of failure: early school leaving and the fact that a significant proportion of students finish compulsory education without having acquired the necessary foundation skills to enter successfully into the labour market. But, paradoxically, obtaining reliable data on these phenomena – that are nationally representative and/or internationally comparable – is particularly difficult.

Early school leavers may drop out of school without finishing a course of study; or they may finish the course but leave without the relevant qualifications. National data of OECD countries show the magnitude of both of these problems.

Three measures of drop-out

The age at which compulsory schooling ends in OECD countries varies between 14 and 18. Even if young people's risks on the labour market cannot be related only to whether they complete compulsory schooling, participation in and completion of upper secondary education are becoming increasingly important.

---

6.   This conclusion is based on a comparison of the data from the three IEA studies on mathematics (1966, 1981 and 1995) and science (1970, 1986 and 1995).

7.   A comparison of students who speak a second language at home with "native speaking" students shows that the "non-native speakers" are likely to come from backgrounds that are more socio-economically disadvantaged, according to the IEA Reading Literacy Study and TIMSS.

Figure 4.4

Three measures of drop-out

Percentage of age-group not enrolled at a particular age

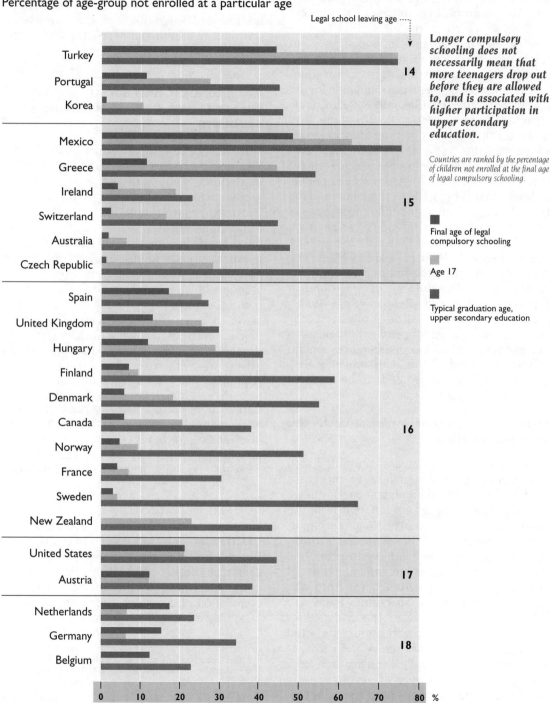

Legal school leaving age ----

Longer compulsory schooling does not necessarily mean that more teenagers drop out before they are allowed to, and is associated with higher participation in upper secondary education.

Countries are ranked by the percentage of children not enrolled at the final age of legal compulsory schooling.

■ Final age of legal compulsory schooling

▨ Age 17

■ Typical graduation age, upper secondary education

Source: OECD Education Database.

Data and notes for Figure 4.4: page 112.

Figure 4.4 looks at three alternative measures of drop-out: the proportion of young people who are not enrolled at the compulsory leaving age; the proportion not participating at the age of 17, when upper secondary education is normally underway; and the proportion not participating at the expected year of upper secondary completion.

Double enrolments can lead to double counting of students and, in a few cases, to apparent rates of above 100 per cent. Despite these imperfections of data, two general conclusions can be drawn:

- Higher leaving ages are not systematically associated with higher drop-out. Enrolment rates tend everywhere to be between 90 and 100 per cent up to the final age of legal compulsory schooling, with the exception of the United States, where it is close to 80 per cent, and Mexico and Turkey, where it is around 50 per cent. Although drop-out is low in the two countries with the lowest final compulsory age, for the other countries there is no discernible relationship between the age at which young people are allowed to leave school and the rate at which they drop out before that age.

- Enrolment drops after the final compulsory school leaving age in almost all countries, albeit to markedly varying degrees. Higher leaving ages appear to be associated with higher participation throughout upper secondary education. Although the proportion remaining in school until the age of 17 or 18 can exceed 80 or 90 per cent even in countries where the leaving age is 16 or below, the evidence shows that education systems with a higher upper limit tend to succeed in keeping more young people at school until the end of upper secondary education. This could argue for raising the age for completing compulsory education in those countries where it is lowest.

However, data on students' reasons for leaving school before finishing their studies make it evident that the extension of compulsory schooling can only have a limited effect. Recent findings from the International Adult Literacy Survey (OECD and Statistics Canada, 1997) show

that approximately twice as many drop-outs cite reasons over which they had no control (institutional pressures, economic need or family reasons) as those who say they left school out of personal choice (lack of interest in education or desire to take up employment).

Curriculum reform has been used to address the drop-out problem. Some OECD countries have attempted to make school more attractive to students, by widening learning opportunities and adopting a more participatory approach to lessons through a change to the ethos or objectives of the curriculum. The purpose has been helping schools to cater for a larger diversity of students' abilities, interests, concerns and career paths. An example of the latter is the recent attempt to reform the Japanese curriculum, initiated in response to concerns that excessive rigidity, narrowness of curriculum and rigid teaching style were demotivating students and even causing some to drop out of the upper secondary system.

Experience in OECD countries shows the importance of two other measures for the prevention of dropping out of school: facilitating transitions and pathways throughout the school system, and improving educational and career guidance. While the transition from school to work has become a main policy focus in most OECD countries, a greater effort is required to facilitate other transitions throughout the schooling process, especially those between pre-school and primary education, and between primary and secondary school. And provision of better guidance services is particularly important in the case of the least advantaged students (for a detailed discussion on this topic, see OECD, 1996*b*).

Unqualified school leavers

Some idea of the size of the "qualification deficiency" among early school leavers is given by comparative data on graduation rates in upper secondary education (see Figure 5.2a). As in the case of drop-out data, these figures have to be interpreted with caution, since definitions of "graduation" vary among OECD Member countries. Furthermore, grade repetition may distort the statistics since the "graduation rate" is measured at the theoretical age of graduation, as a per cent of the total school population at that age. Additionally, in some countries, and especially in those with apprenticeship training programmes, students may gain more than one upper secondary qualification, which may lead to apparent completion rates of over 100 per cent.

Even allowing for these caveats, available data reflect a wide range of upper secondary graduation rates, from under 40 per cent in Mexico and Turkey to over 90 per cent in a range of countries: Belgium, Finland, Ireland, Japan, New Zealand and Norway (see Table G1.1, Indicator G1 in the companion volume, *Education at a Glance*). An equally wide variation between countries is found if one compares general and vocational qualifications. No relationship can therefore be established between graduation rates and the type of educational programme. But female graduation rates do seem to be slightly higher than rates for men; probably because men on average tend to enter the labour market earlier. However, high unemployment rates or relatively low earnings for those having attained less than a full cycle of secondary education suggest that these non-graduate men are likely to be economically at risk. One may therefore conclude that *young people with no qualifications will be almost as vulnerable, economically and socially, as those who drop out*.

Having said that, it must be emphasised that the level of qualification needed to enter the labour market is defined – to a considerable extent – by employers' perceptions and expectations. And employers' views of what constitutes an adequate level of qualification have undergone a seemingly permanent upward shift since the early 1970s, as confirmed by a recent comparative study of the Netherlands, Ireland and the United Kingdom (Hannan *et al.*, 1995). It is therefore important to stress that what constitutes an "appropriate" qualification is a "moving target", and hence a problem that cannot be addressed by schools alone.

Young adults with inadequate foundation skills

However easy or difficult their passage through school, and whether or not they obtain a qualification, a certain number of students finish compulsory education without having acquired the foundation skills necessary for their social and productive integration into modern society. Some idea of the link between inadequate skills and labour market status is provided by results from the International Adult Literacy Survey (IALS). The literacy skills of those surveyed were graded on a rising five point scale, within which skill Levels 1 and 2 were judged inadequate to meet the demands of modern life and, in particular, the needs of the knowledge economy (see Chapter 3 for further details).

In the 12 OECD countries so far covered by the IALS, there is a substantial proportion of young people (16-29 year olds) who lack the literacy skills necessary to ensure their social and economic integration. The proportion of this age-group scoring at the bottom two levels is between 35 and 38 per cent in a cluster of four countries, with extremes of 18 per cent in the highest achieving country, and 66 per cent in the lowest (see OECD, 1996*b*, p. 72). There is also evidence that successive cohorts tend to record better literacy scores (i.e. the 16-29 year-olds do better than the 30-65 year-olds).

The IALS results show that young people with poor literacy skills are more likely to be unemployed than those with better skills (OECD and Statistics Canada, 1995 and 1997). In Canada, Ireland and the United States, young adults with poor skills have unemployment rates twice those of youth with high skills. In the Netherlands and the United Kingdom the differences are even larger (Figure 4.5). Even for those people with low skills who do find jobs, they will not necessarily be stable, rewarding or well-paid. Figure 4.5 illustrates this point for five countries for which the sample sizes are sufficient to give significant results. Even though the majority of young people in the labour force with low literacy levels are in work, they are more likely than those with high skills to have low income. The prospects of holding well-paid jobs increases with rising literacy, although not equally steeply in all countries. For workers with low literacy skills, the prospect of holding a better paid job varies among countries. In the United States, they are 31/2 times as likely to be in the worst-paid 40 per cent of all workers – for those whose pay is known. In other countries shown, with the

Figure 4.5
Literacy, employment and incomes among young people
Percentage of 16-35 year-olds in the labour force at low and high document literacy levels who are:

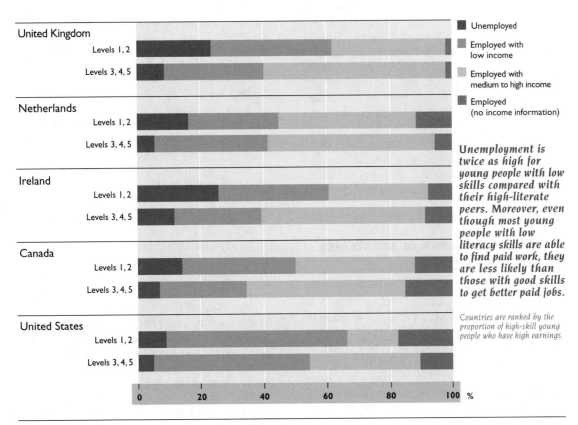

Legend:
- Unemployed
- Employed with low income
- Employed with medium to high income
- Employed (no income information)

Unemployment is twice as high for young people with low skills compared with their high-literate peers. Moreover, even though most young people with low literacy skills are able to find paid work, they are less likely than those with good skills to get better paid jobs.

Countries are ranked by the proportion of high-skill young people who have high earnings.

Source: OECD and Statistics Canada, International Adult Literacy Survey.
Data and notes for Figure 4.5: page 113.

exception of the Netherlands, the chances are about even for young adults with low literacy skills to have low or high income, but there is a clear earnings advantage for their high-literate peers.

The data presented in the previous chapter indicated that there is a strong correlation between possession of adequate levels of literacy (IALS Level 3 and above) and completion of upper secondary education (ISCED Level 3 and above). Therefore, the risk of marginalisation is no longer confined to those who have failed to complete primary or lower secondary education. In most countries, a completed upper secondary education appears to have become the norm.

The IALS results also show (see Chapter 3, this volume, and OECD, 1996d, Chapter 2) that:

• Young adults with poor qualifications and skills, who need additional education more than most, are the least likely to engage in further learning; and

• People with higher levels of education are more likely to, but by no means certain to, demonstrate good literacy skills. In particular, people with upper secondary education show highly variable patterns of literacy across countries. This result implies that failure to acquire skills cannot be looked at narrowly in terms of school performance.

Accordingly, as well as reinforcing the need to address the problem of early school leaving, these indicators call into question the real value of the qualifications obtained by upper secondary school graduates. They justify the efforts undertaken in some countries (for example, Germany, the Netherlands, the United Kingdom and the United States) to specify more closely the standards or levels of skills young people need to have attained by the time they complete a full cycle of secondary education. Finally, they strengthen the case for improving the quality of initial schooling, since the early years of education have been found to be crucial not only for foundation learning, but also for further learning, especially in the case of disadvantaged children (OECD, 1996c).

4.5 KEY INGREDIENTS OF STRATEGIES TO IMPROVE SCHOOLING

Whatever the form in which failure appears in diverse educational cultures, policy-makers in OECD countries face a common challenge in improving the strategies for tackling this problem. In order to do so, they need to consider four key issues: i) early recognition, early action; ii) combating failure on a wide front; iii) flexible approaches to student needs; and iv) learning from the experience of others.

i) Labelling a student or a school as "failing" can worsen the problem, because it can stigmatise the individual or the institution. Some countries therefore prefer to emphasise the "success" of students and schools. In contrast, the argument advanced in those countries where "failing" schools are publicly identified is that such an approach delivers a "shock" necessary in order to galvanise some schools into action. Views vary with culture, and with differences in educational organisation. But every country in its own way needs to face up to the indicators in this chapter that show that a substantial proportion of young adults do not possess the knowledge and skills needed for work. Regardless of whether policies for reducing failure are framed in "positive" or "negative" terms, acceptance of the problem is the necessary prelude to developing policies for helping students and schools. And action at an early rather than a late stage will make intervention more effective.

ii) Failure is the result of the interaction of many variables: some depend on the students themselves, some relate to factors in their home and community environment, and others are school-based (inappropriate teaching methods, inadequate resources, poor curriculum). It is now widely accepted that no single explanation can account satisfactorily for educational failure. This realisation has led to the development of a broad range of policies – systemic, institutional and programmatic – to address the different facets and contexts of failure. To be most effective, such policies need the support of different actors involved in education: parents and students themselves; school leaders and teachers; social workers and educational authorities. Inter-agency co-operation, as well as the collaboration of schools, families and communities are required to create appropriate frameworks for supporting children at risk, from birth through to their integration into the workplace (OECD, 1995, p. 144).

iii) In the 21st century, success at school will no longer be measured by the number of years studied nor by the attainment of a diploma for life. Rather, students will be expected to complete successfully different learning itineraries and to acquire the motivation to engage in lifelong learning. This will require a more flexible curriculum; smoother transition points throughout the schooling process; less rigid forms of evaluation and certification; and a pedagogy which meets the needs of all students (OECD, 1996c). The implications for teacher training – both initial and in-service – are considerable since the role and function of the teacher have to be conceptualised in a new way. Teachers cannot continue to be mere "knowledge transmitters" who help the students to obtain an upper secondary qualification. Rather, the teacher has to support students so that they can successfully complete diverse learning pathways and continue learning throughout a lifetime.

iv) Disseminating best practice requires effective monitoring and evaluation of "what works". But very few of the policies attempted to overcome failure have been systematically monitored or fully evaluated. Furthermore, comparative indicators of failure are scanty, in part because the problem is defined differently in different countries. Thus, an effort must be made to develop a comparative knowledge base on educational failure and success, both at the national and the international levels.

4.6 CONCLUSIONS

As a result of rapid technological innovation and restructuring in labour markets, the foundation skills which all individuals need for their social and productive integration have become more complex. The analysis presented in this chapter suggests that the greatest risks of marginalisation, unemployment or low income are no longer confined to those who have failed to complete primary or lower secondary schooling. In most OECD countries, it now seems that it is not until young people have attained at least upper secondary education that their chances of finding employment with adequate pay significantly improve. Providing all students with a full cycle of secondary education will thus have to become the norm, and school and student failure and success will have to be assessed against this benchmark. ■

References

BEATON, A.E., MULLIS, I.V.S., MARTIN, M.O., GONZALES, E.J., KELLY, D.L. and SMITH, T.A. (1996), *Mathematics Achievement in the Middle School Years*, TIMSS International Study Center, Boston College, Chestnut Hill, MA.

ELLEY, W.B. (1992), *How in the World do Students Read?*, Grindeldruck GMBH, Hamburg.

HANNAN, D., HÖVELS, B., VAN DER BERG, S. and WHITE, M. (1995), "Early leavers from education and training in Ireland, the Netherlands and the United Kingdom", *European Journal of Education*, Vol. 30(3), pp. 325-347.

MARTIN, M.O., MULLIS, I.V.S., BEATON, A.E., GONZALES, E.J., SMITH, T.A. and KELLY, D.L. (1997), *Science Achievement in the Primary School Years*, TIMSS International Study Center, Boston College, Chestnut Hill, MA.

MULLIS, I.V.S., MARTIN, M.O., BEATON, A.E., GONZALES, E.J., KELLY, D.L. and SMITH, T.A. (1997), *Mathematics Achievement in the Primary School Years*, TIMSS International Study Center, Boston College, Chestnut Hill, MA.

OECD (1994), *The OECD Jobs Study*, Paris.

OECD (1995), *Our Children at Risk*, Paris.

OECD (1996a), "Combating failure at school: A report on the activity", Paris.

OECD (1996b), *Mapping the Future: Young People and Career Guidance*, Paris.

OECD (1996c), *Lifelong Learning for All*, Paris.

OECD (1996d) *Education at a Glance: Analysis*, Paris.

OECD (1997), *Education and Equity in OECD Countries*, Paris.

OECD and STATISTICS CANADA (1995), *Literacy, Economy and Society: Results of the First International Adult Literacy Survey*, Paris and Ottawa.

OECD and STATISTICS CANADA (1997), *Literacy Skills for the Knowledge Society: Further Results of the First International Adult Literacy Survey*, Paris and Ottawa.

CHAPTER 5

RESPONDING TO NEW DEMAND IN TERTIARY EDUCATION

SUMMARY

A growing number of young people, and increasingly adults as well, are participating in tertiary education. The expansion in the first years of tertiary education has to a large extent been driven by demand – by the desire of a wider group of people to be educated to higher levels, together with a growth in the acquisition of upper secondary and other qualifications that gain them access. New groups bring new interests and needs, which oblige tertiary systems to diversify structures, programmes and styles of delivery. This chapter looks at where the new demand is coming from, at how systems and institutions are responding, and at the degree to which they are able to offer suitable courses that lead to completion rather than drop-out.

A continuing rise in demand can be seen not only in countries where tertiary education has expanded relatively recently, but also in those where it has been growing for some time. But new demand is coming from a greater range of age groups; even among people in their late twenties, participation rates are above 10 per cent in Denmark, Finland, Germany, Norway and the United States. Students therefore come to tertiary education with a wide range of prior experiences. They enter tertiary education programmes with either academic or vocational qualifications acquired in upper secondary education, often with some other post-compulsory or tertiary education experience as well and sometimes with validated experience gained outside educational institutions. This range of student background adds to the diversity of their interests and needs.

An increased number of students come from relatively disadvantaged backgrounds, although their share in the total student body does not appear to have risen markedly. A more dramatic change is in the number of women, who now comprise a majority of students in most countries.

As a result of these changes in demand, the character of tertiary education and of students' experiences is evolving. Three features are particularly notable:

- The widening of vocational or professional studies, whether through new "non-university" programmes or institutions or changes in the curricula of existing study programmes;

- The opening up by institutions of alternative pathways, particularly in countries where students have previously been channelled in pre-set directions within highly segmented systems;

- The opening up of such pathways by the students themselves, who are making new kinds of choices and thus creating new norms.

In managing these changes, an important challenge facing tertiary institutions is to reduce the incidence of inefficient routes and drop-out. Although non-completion is a big concern for many countries, it is difficult to measure how many students leave tertiary education for negative reasons, how many never intended to complete a full degree or diploma, and how many go on to complete tertiary courses other than those in which they enrolled initially.

Thus governments face the challenge of encouraging the development of diverse and flexible options which are clear in expectations, outcomes and links. Students need to be able to find courses that are well suited to their capacities, interests and needs. This greater flexibility has to be balanced with good information, guidance and structured programmes to ensure that learning efforts are not wasted.

5.1 INTRODUCTION

Tertiary education traditionally has educated an elite group of young people to higher levels immediately after they complete upper secondary education. Today, it provides opportunities for learning to a much larger section of the youth and adult population. Figure 5.1 indicates that tertiary institutions now reach a quarter to a third of people in their late teens and early twenties in a number of countries, and in some cases over 10 per cent of the population are enrolled even in their late twenties. This expansion has been driven primarily by demand from a wider and more diverse group of people for study beyond secondary schooling, as a result of social and economic developments common to all OECD countries. The challenge for tertiary education systems is not merely to meet demand with an expansion of places, but also to adapt programmes, and teaching and learning to match a more diverse set of student needs while also meeting the needs of the economy and society.

This final chapter looks at the structure of the demand, at how systems are responding and at the degree to which they are succeeding in meeting new needs and interests. It focuses on the first years of tertiary education (see Box 5A). Specifically, the chapter addresses the following questions:

- How much has demand risen?
- What are the routes into tertiary education?
- What is the profile of today's entrants?
- What kinds of option are being offered to these students?
- How many entrants fail to "complete" a first cycle of tertiary education, and how can drop-out be avoided?

These questions pose some clear challenges for policy makers. A system that caters for an increasingly heterogeneous group of students must work not only to develop its diversity, but also to ensure that students are in practice offered a range of choices that they can match to their needs. However, diversity and choice are not without limits. Students need to be

helped to acquire a complex range of advanced-level knowledge, skills and dispositions. They cannot do so simply by choosing from a vast, undifferentiated array of course options. The key role of institutions is their ability to organise learning in ways that reflect the complex structures of knowledge, its uses and the interrelationships among its elements. The challenge is how to provide for diversity and choice while ensuring the effectiveness and efficiency of well-designed, coherent programmes.

A further policy challenge is to address the needs of the economy and of society alongside individual demands. The OECD *Jobs Study* (1994) signalled the imperative of improving flexibility in the population to foster economic growth and employment. That flexibility can be partly realised through a progressive implementation of a lifelong approach to learning as set out by OECD Education Ministers (OECD, 1996a). But governments cannot expect to promote strategies for lifelong learning by directly controlling tertiary education. On the contrary, there is a need to build up the capacity of institutions to manage themselves and to forge new partnerships with employers and others, to help meet economic and social demands. An important requirement of these new partnerships is to move beyond a view of graduates as people with homogeneous attributes and knowledge, and beyond a single narrow conception of what a first degree or diploma should certify. This does not mean abandoning standards or quality control. Rather, within and among the diverse range of learning options, each study programme needs to have well-defined standards, content and qualifications. The characteristics of programmes should be made transparent to employers and others, and students should be able to move more flexibly among them.

5.2 THE RISE IN DEMAND

New demand for tertiary education has come from a variety of sources. Rising aspirations, changing patterns of employment and careers and rising incomes and wealth have made some continuation of education beyond the secondary level both an expectation and a perceived

Box 5A
WHAT IS MEANT BY THE FIRST YEARS OF TERTIARY EDUCATION?

Tertiary education refers to a level of broadly defined studies, provided through established forms of higher education, but also in other ways – through new kinds of institutions, by enterprises and in other non-formal settings.

Nevertheless, it is mainly through institutions – colleges, polytechnics, universities, whether public or private – that tertiary education is provided.

The *first years of tertiary education*, the subject of this chapter, refer to the period of study (typically three to five years) undertaken prior to the award of an initial qualification that is recognised on the labour market. Adult education, in a wide variety of forms, is generally excluded from this definition, as are programmes that lead primarily to awards at sub-degree level.

An element of imprecision is inevitable, given the different structural arrangements in Member countries and the choices students themselves make. See OECD (1997b).

necessity for a growing number of individuals. At the same time, a more educated population is collectively considered an important investment for societies and economies (see Chapter 2).

It is not possible to calculate precisely the demand for tertiary education in societies where most of its participants are dependent on supply decisions made by governments. Nevertheless, the rate of enrolment in tertiary education is one proxy measure of demand, since decisions to provide places are influenced by pressure from those who wish to participate. Another indirect measure is the rate at which people qualify to enter tertiary education by graduating from upper secondary programmes.

Figure 5.1 indicates that demand continues to grow not only in countries where rapid expansion occurred relatively recently, such as France, Portugal and Norway, but also in those with longer experience of high levels of participation such as Canada and the United States. But the age range at which enrolment rates are rising fastest varies from one country to another. In France, for example, the biggest growth from the mid-1980s to the mid-1990s was for the age group 18-21: the enrolment rate for this group rose from one-fifth to one-third of the total. But in the United States, one-third of the population aged 18-21 were already enrolled by 1985, and the growth in demand came rather from people in their mid-twenties. Higher participation among older age groups in some countries reflects a lengthening of the duration of studies, but it can also indicate more frequent alternation between work and study, or a growth in combined or complementary qualifications. All these possibilities add to the diversity of demand that tertiary education must respond to.

Since 1980 the proportion of young people who complete a full cycle of secondary education, and therefore qualify (in most cases) for entrance into tertiary education, has increased in all countries (see OECD, 1996b, p.15). By 1995, the proportion of the cohort completing upper secondary education exceeded 90 per cent in Belgium (Flemish Community), Finland, Ireland, Japan, New Zealand, and Norway (see Figure 5.2).

This increase in completion of upper secondary education tends to lead to higher participation in tertiary education independently of policies adopted for that sector. Once learning is realised on this scale in upper secondary education, it is hard to resist the consequent demand for tertiary studies – particularly in countries that offer a specific entitlement to further study to upper secondary-school graduates. In countries such as Australia, Denmark, France and Ireland, policies to increase the proportion of the age cohort completing secondary education have not only succeeded in achieving that objective but also led directly to a rise in the numbers entering tertiary programmes.

Figure 5.1
Trends in participation in tertiary education by age
Percentage of three age groups enrolled in tertiary education, public and private, 1985 and 1995

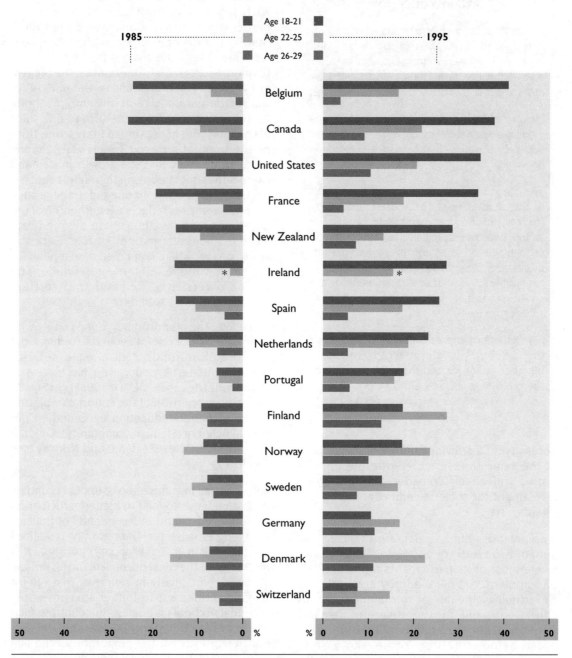

* Data refer to ages 22-29.
Source: OECD Education Database.
Data and notes for Figure 5.1: page 114.

More young people are participating in tertiary education than before: not just teenagers, but in many countries, a substantial proportion of people in their early and late twenties.

Countries are ranked by the net enrolment rates of 18-21 year-olds in 1995.

Figure 5.2a
Routes to upper secondary graduation
Ratio of upper secondary graduates to population at typical graduation age,
by type of programme and gender, 1995

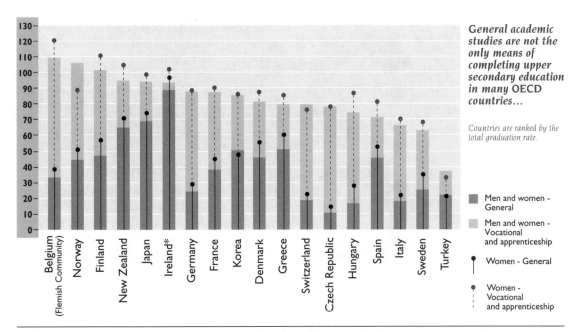

General academic studies are not the only means of completing upper secondary education in many OECD countries...

Countries are ranked by the total graduation rate.

■ Men and women - General

■ Men and women - Vocational and apprenticeship

● Women - General

● Women - Vocational and apprenticeship

* "General" upper secondary education contains a number of strong vocational elements.   *Data for Figure 5.2a: page 114.*
Source: OECD Education Database.

However, it should not be taken for granted that upper secondary completion will continue steadily to rise. In the United States, for example, completion rates appear to have stabilised or decreased to levels below 80 per cent. But this does not automatically reduce the demand for tertiary study. While the proportion of US public high school students estimated to graduate fell from 73 per cent in 1986 to 70 per cent in 1994, the proportion who went on to participate in tertiary education rose sharply, from 43 per cent to 57 per cent (Mortenson, 1996).[1]

In France, the number of those attaining the *baccalauréat* increased strongly to 1995 (a doubling over 10 years), but is expected to remain at present levels, about 60 per cent of the cohort, to 2005. While some French young people who lack this upper secondary school qualification pursue other forms of vocationally-qualifying education, an estimated 20 per cent of the cohort are expected to be students who

present themselves for the *baccalauréat*, but do not pass. Both the French and US cases thus illustrate a widespread and worrying polarisation between a greater number continuing on to tertiary studies and a substantial number failing during the course of secondary schooling (see also Chapter 4).

5.3 ROUTES INTO TERTIARY EDUCATION

Expansion in the number of young people completing either academic or vocational streams of upper secondary education explains only partly the increase in demand for tertiary education. There is also growing use of alternative routes and pathways for young people and adults who have some post-

1.   The estimates for high school completion are based on public high school students who subsequently graduate; those for enrolment in tertiary education cover both public and private high school graduates.

Figure 5.2b
Routes to tertiary education
Qualifications on entry in selected countries,
percentage distributions, various years

*... and between one
in seven and nearly
one in two students
enter tertiary-level
programmes with
qualifications
other than or
in addition to
general upper
secondary education.*

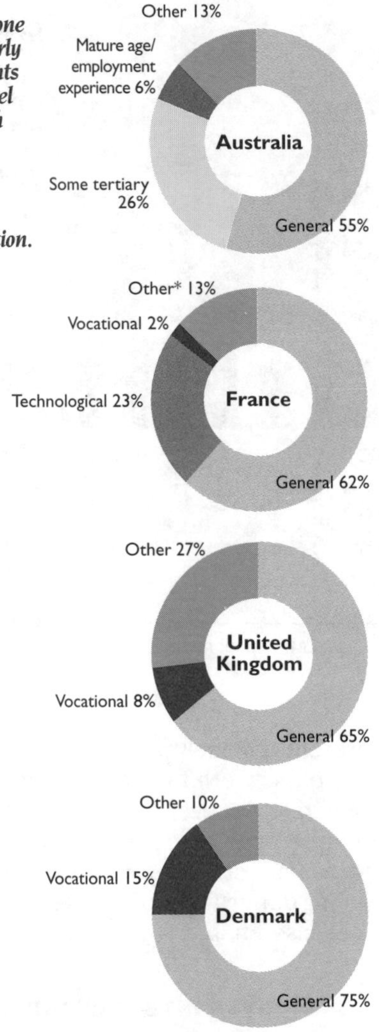

Other 13%
Mature age/
employment
experience 6%
Australia
Some tertiary
26%
General 55%

Other* 13%
Vocational 2%
Technological 23%
France
General 62%

Other 27%
**United
Kingdom**
Vocational 8%
General 65%

Other 10%
Vocational 15%
Denmark
General 75%

Vocational 15%
Japan
General 85%

*Countries are ranked by the percentage
of new entrants with other than general
secondary educational qualifications.*

* Other includes students with a *baccalauréat* who changed
programmes as well as students with some tertiary experience.
Data, notes and sources for Figure 5.2b: page 115.

compulsory or tertiary education experience. A growing number of entrants are adults who have long since left secondary school, many of whom use such alternative routes in.

Figure 5.2a shows that among those who complete an upper secondary programme, in some countries a large proportion do so through vocational and apprenticeship routes. This is partly reflected in the background of those who enter tertiary education. But, as indicated in Figure 5.2b, students entering tertiary education programmes may have prior experience in tertiary education or enter through other routes such as conversion courses, professional qualifications and on the basis of work experience.

In Denmark, for example, about a quarter of entrants into tertiary education come through upper secondary vocational education or non-traditional routes of access. In France, about one-sixth of first year enrolments in tertiary education have qualifications other than the general or technological *baccalauréat*; a large proportion of these students have switched from other tertiary-level programmes, bringing additional educational experience to their first year studies. In Australia, only just over half of those commencing bachelor's courses are admitted on the basis of the completion of the final year of secondary education. Of the remainder, over half have already undertaken a previous tertiary course, and are likely to have different needs from those who have just left secondary education. In the United Kingdom, more than one third of full-time, first degree and diploma students present qualifications other than A-Levels; the Council for Industry and Higher Education (CIHE) advocates that eventually A-Level qualifications (the "academic" route) should account for about half of entrants into tertiary education, with the other half comprised primarily of those with General National Vocational Qualifications (GNVQ).

Any policies addressing routes of access to tertiary education need to consider people's needs over their whole life rather than just at the point of leaving secondary school. As discussed in the next section, in some countries around half of new entrants into tertiary education are aged over 25. The routes by which these adults qualify can no longer be seen as a side issue, but will influence the mission and character of the entire system.

5.4 THE PROFILE OF NEW ENTRANTS

People entering tertiary education come from a wide range of social backgrounds. Over time, the characteristics of those aspiring to tertiary-level studies have grown more diverse as a result of changes in policy aims, in levels of provision of post-compulsory education, in social welfare policies and in employment conditions and prospects. Three patterns in the profile of new entrants in particular should be noted:

Tertiary education caters for all social and ethnic backgrounds, despite a continuing bias towards privileged socio-economic groups.

A significant, although under-representative, group of students in tertiary education come from less privileged socio-economic backgrounds. The number, if not the share, of students from these groups has increased with expansion in most countries. There are no reliable and internationally comparable indicators on the social pattern of enrolment. But within countries, there is a tendency for working-class participation to be substantially greater (but still under-representative) on courses of brief rather than long duration and with a vocational rather than general orientation.

In Denmark, for example, a longitudinal study following the experiences of a cohort aged 14 in 1968 showed that by age 38, only 14 per cent of those who pursued long-cycle studies had "working-class" origins, compared to 30 per cent of students on short-cycle courses. But since 37 per cent of the survey population was classified as working class, this group was under-represented even on short-cycle courses. The professional class, constituting 7 per cent of the survey population, was slightly over-represented on short-cycle courses (8 per cent of students) and greatly over-represented in long-cycle studies (29 per cent).[2]

But has large-volume participation narrowed the gap between high and low socio-economic groups? The evidence is mixed.

- In the United States, differentials have actually widened since the 1970s. Between 1977-79 and 1991-93, the participation rate of 18- and 19-year-olds from families in the top income quartile rose from 69 per cent to 75 per cent, while that of young people from the bottom quartile remained stable at 26 per cent (Kane, 1995).

- In Japan, the trend is less clear-cut: from 1980 to 1990 the share of student enrolment by young people originating from the bottom two income quintiles remained constant, but in the previous decade they had increased their share from 27 per cent to 36 per cent of tertiary enrolments (excluding special training schools) (Kaneko and Kitamura, 1995).

Many factors influence the participation of people from less privileged backgrounds. An increasing number of young people and adults from these groups participate in a widening range of post-compulsory education and training options instead of regular tertiary education studies. New teaching styles throughout the education system can help to make such studies more accessible to potential learners from some socio-economic groups than they have been in the past.

But as countries such as Australia, Italy, the Netherlands, New Zealand, Portugal and the United Kingdom introduce or consider policies requiring greater student (as well as third-party) contributions to meet part of the cost of tertiary education, there is a risk that those from less advantaged groups will be more reluctant to enrol. To attack the perception of unaffordability, current budget proposals in the United States would provide tax breaks introducing a transparent, federal "guarantee" of public funding sufficient to meet minimum tuition charges for anyone who aspires to and is able to benefit from tertiary education. The United States and other countries with tuition fees are seeking to reduce further the risk of weaker participation among lower socio-economic groups through the allocation of need-based financial support, or by postponement or forgiveness of repayment, when the incomes of graduates fall short of a given threshold.

---

2. For the purposes of the study, "professional class" comprises all who function in knowledge-based positions, including engineers; teachers and librarians; doctors, veterinary surgeons and dentists, and architects. See Hansen (1996).

Figure 5.3a
Women entering tertiary education
As a percentage of new entrants, 1995

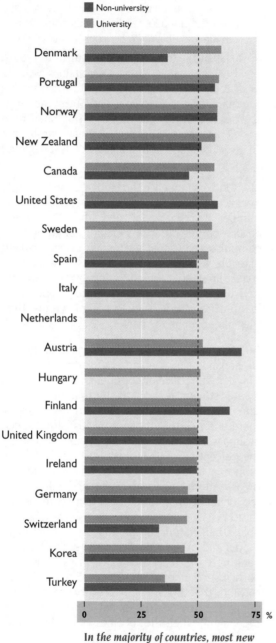

■ Non-university
■ University

Denmark
Portugal
Norway
New Zealand
Canada
United States
Sweden
Spain
Italy
Netherlands
Austria
Hungary
Finland
United Kingdom
Ireland
Germany
Switzerland
Korea
Turkey

0   25   50   75 %

In the majority of countries, most new students are women...

Countries are ranked by entry into university education.

Source: OECD Education Database.
Data for Figure 5.3a: page 115.

For reasons specific to the countries concerned, New Zealand and the United States have supported the development of separate, publicly-funded tertiary-level institutions to cater for specific needs and interests of some young people and adults from identified minority groups (respectively, Maori, and Native American and African American). Students from these groups already can be found in significant numbers in the programmes and institutions aimed at all young people and adults, but their overall participation rates remain relatively low.

Women are now a majority of participants in tertiary education, although their representation differs greatly by course type.

If the change in the social balance in tertiary education has been at best limited, the change in the gender balance has been dramatic. Figure 5.3a shows that, in a majority of OECD countries, most students enrolled are now women.

The growth in women's participation has been stimulated by high upper secondary school completion rates, particularly from general streams, which in a number of countries are more likely to lead to tertiary education. Indeed, in all but two of the 18 countries shown in Figure 5.2a, women are more likely than men to complete secondary school in general streams (exceptions are Korea and Turkey). In some countries, this appears to be because men are more likely to follow vocational options, as in Norway, where 50 per cent of women and 38 per cent of men graduate from general courses. In others, the gender difference is apparent even though there is relatively little vocational education. An example is Ireland, where 96 per cent of women but 83 per cent of men complete general streams in upper secondary.

The gender balance varies widely in different fields of study. The programmes least likely to enrol women are those in natural sciences and in industrial and engineering fields. Women are more likely to enrol in fields related to the health professions, education and in the social and behavioural sciences (Figure 5.3b). In some countries, study programmes in the latter fields are found outside universities, and often limit enrolment in line with capacity constraints and estimates by public authorities of needed or desired supply of highly-qualified labour. The consequence,

Figure 5.3b
The gender balance in different subjects
Percentage of new entrants who are women, selected subjects, 1995

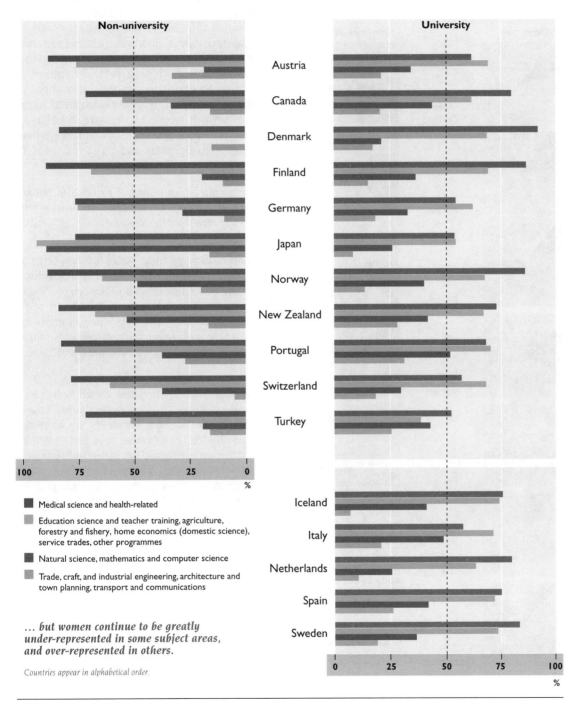

Medical science and health-related

Education science and teacher training, agriculture, forestry and fishery, home economics (domestic science), service trades, other programmes

Natural science, mathematics and computer science

Trade, craft, and industrial engineering, architecture and town planning, transport and communications

... but women continue to be greatly under-represented in some subject areas, and over-represented in others.

Countries appear in alphabetical order.

Source: OECD Education Database.
Data for Figure 5.3b: page 116.

Figure 5.4
**First-time entrants into
tertiary education by age, 1995**

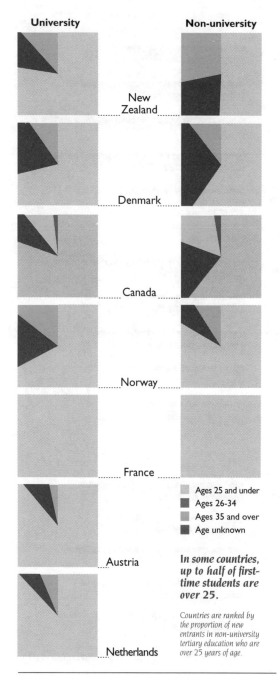

University   Non-university

New
Zealand

Denmark

Canada

Norway

France

Ages 25 and under
Ages 26-34
Ages 35 and over
Age unknown

Austria

*In some countries,
up to half of first-
time students are
over 25.*

*Countries are ranked by
the proportion of new
entrants in non-university
tertiary education who are
over 25 years of age.*

Netherlands

The surface represented by each square is equal in size to
the estimated values provided in the corresponding table.
Source: OECD Education Database.
Data and notes for Figure 5.4: page 116.

in Denmark for example, is that young women may be less likely than young men to enter or succeed in their first choice programme or institution. Conversely, young women represent a significant reservoir of intellectual talent which could be brought into science, mathematics and technical programmes in tertiary education where capacity exceeds enrolment. This is a particularly attractive possibility in countries where the number of graduates in these subjects is considered to fall short of what is needed to undergird balanced medium-term economic development. Steps have been taken, in Denmark and other countries, to influence women's choices.

In some countries up to half of entrants to tertiary education are over age 25, although this varies greatly according to each country's situation.

Adult participation is creating a "quiet" revolution in tertiary student profiles. Figure 5.4 shows that, in a few countries, nearly half of students enter tertiary education for the first time after the age of 25. But this is by no means a general trend. In some countries, fewer than one in five new entrants are over 25; these include Austria and the Netherlands. In France, virtually all new entrants are under 25 years of age.

Where adult participation has grown, it has to a large extent done so because individuals have preferred to delay entry, because they wanted a "second chance" or because they felt that they needed to upgrade their skills, rather than because governments have followed specific policies to get adults to study. But in some cases such policies have indeed played a role: during the 1980s, Sweden's "25:4" scheme, which reserved tertiary education places for those at least 25 years of age and with four years of work experience, assured greater adult participation than had previously been the case. Australia and the United Kingdom have for some years had special admissions schemes for mature age students. These countries and Japan also offer open university programmes. In New Zealand, policy has long provided a favourable, "open admissions" route for adults. Indeed, the growth in adult enrolments has so raised concerns about rates of admission of younger New Zealanders that the government has put in place a "study-right" incentive for providers through which an increased level of public funding is provided to institutions for each student *under* 22 who enrols in tertiary education for the first time.

The reasons why adults in some countries participate so much less than in others are complex, reflecting country structures and traditions. The extensive provision of vocational education and apprenticeships in Austria, Belgium, Denmark, Germany, the Netherlands and Switzerland has provided solid preparation and qualification for work and so reduced the perceived need to acquire formal tertiary-level studies at a later date. In these countries, many adults already participate in job-related education and training, outside formal institutions, as well as other forms of learning. The pattern may be changing, however, as growing numbers of young people with post-compulsory vocational qualifications seek to enter tertiary education: in Germany, an estimated 40 per cent of those participating in vocational training in the dual system eventually take up tertiary studies.

It is possible that the age distribution of learners will widen further as tertiary education becomes more open and accessible to all students, regardless of age. Such an opening up provides learners with greater scope to determine the best timing for their entry into tertiary education.

5.5 SUPPLY-SIDE RESPONSES

In response to large-volume participation and to new kinds of demand for tertiary education, a wide range of options have been developed. Diversification has taken a number of forms both within and outside tertiary institutions. It has included more "non-university" institutions and programmes, a blurring of the distinctiveness of programmes between sectors, better articulation between courses, the networking of institutions and programmes, "franchise" arrangements or distance learning.

One indicator of diversity is the introduction and further development of "non-university" programmes, that serve to broaden the forms of tertiary education available to learners. Figure 5.5 shows that around one half of students in the first years of tertiary education are enrolled in such programmes in certain countries. These pro- grammes give greater emphasis to applications of learning and especially links to employment.

Figure 5.5
The split between university and other tertiary education programmes
Percentage of non-university tertiary education in total enrolment, first stage, 1995

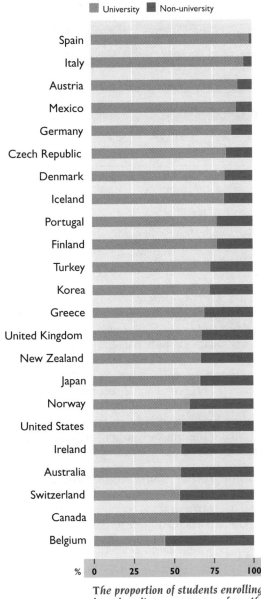

The proportion of students enrolling in university courses ranges from the vast majority in some countries to around half in others.

Countries are ranked by the percentage enrolled in university education.

Source: OECD Education Database.
Data for Figure 5.5: page 117.

Figure 5.6
Entry qualifications and type of programme
Initial destinations in tertiary education, selected countries, various years

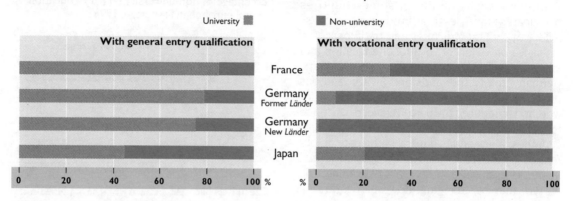

Typically, students with general qualifications enrol in university courses while those with vocational qualifications enrol in other types of programmes. But a substantial proportion follow atypical routes.

Countries are ranked by the proportion with general entry qualifications.

Non-university programmes are particularly attractive to adults, owing to a short programme duration and more flexible organisational arrangements which support part-time, evening, work based and distance learning options. In some cases they have been seen as a tertiary level extension of technical and professional secondary education. Austria, the Czech Republic, Finland, Italy and Mexico have undertaken or are contemplating reforms aimed at developing new distinctive institutions and programmes of this type.

Regardless of the intent of existing structures, there has in practice been a considerable easing of the rigid tracks that in some countries have tended to preclude participation in tertiary education for students from secondary vocational streams, or to channel students from particular secondary streams into associated tertiary branches. Figure 5.6 shows that while some forms of entry qualification are more likely to lead to given types of tertiary education than others, the match is by no means a precise one. In France, for example, while about 85 per cent of those entering tertiary education with the general *baccalauréat* choose university programmes or preparatory classes for the *grandes écoles*, 15 per cent choose the short-cycle, vocationally-

oriented programmes offered through the university institutes of technology (IUT) or the advanced technician sections (STS) of the *lycées*. Conversely, while about 70 per cent of those entering tertiary education with the technological *baccalauréat* choose "matching" forms of tertiary education (IUT and STS), some 30 per cent enrol in university programmes. In Germany and Japan, similar patterns can be observed; for example, about one-fifth of Japanese graduates of the vocational stream of upper secondary education go on to enrol in university programmes.

While such "crossover" can be measured directly in countries where tertiary institutions are segmented into distinct categories, an equivalent growth in flexibility is occurring, if less visibly, in "unitary" systems with a single kind of institution. In both segmented and unitary systems, there is an increasing diversity of programmes and arrangements, within and among institutions, regardless of sector or status. The distinction between university and non-university is blurred almost everywhere. It is common for institutions of different types to offer programmes which might lead to similar jobs, if not providing similar coursework – for example in the

Box 5B
DIVERSIFYING THE SUPPLY OF TERTIARY EDUCATION

Diversity in Sweden's unitary system. Though diverse in character and programmes, all institutions operate under a single framework and on a single funding basis. Diversity and distinctiveness in programmes are maintained and enhanced through a reflection in university colleges of regional interests, and also through productive co-operative working arrangements between, for example, the University of Uppsala and the University College of Örebro in which Uppsala professors work in Örebro. Such co-operative arrangements permit each institution to develop its distinctive character while benefiting students and staff at both.

Extending tertiary provision in New Zealand. Secondary schools may be approved to offer tertiary-level course modules; those that do so typically have established articulation arrangements with nearby universities or polytechnics and may work co-operatively with teaching staff at these institutions. Funding is provided from the government to the secondary school, on the basis of the number of students enrolled.

Bachelor's degree in Denmark. The Ministry approved and has supported the introduction of a three-year bachelor's degree as the first tertiary-level qualification in universities, rather than the most common five-six year master's degree. There is successful experience in engineering and business, and wider acceptance of the degree is being fostered through means such as development of a "vocationally-oriented" six-month module to be attached to bachelor's degree programmes and an experimental linking of basic teacher education with the university to be established in the domain of science.

Work experience in the United Kingdom. The government's Enterprise in Higher Education initiative and the work of Training Enterprise Councils have had the effect of stimulating new active teaching partnerships. Co-operative arrangements enable students to apply what they have learnt in their formal studies in the work environment (often with an assessment and credit for the experience and knowledge gained) and provide a value-added service for the firm or organisation concerned.

New tertiary education option in Switzerland. In the face of reduced volume in apprenticeships, increased demand for tertiary education, and in order to make higher vocational education attractive for better students with practical training, a new upper secondary qualification (*Berufsmaturität*/maturité professionnelle) was introduced. This permits access to the newly created *Fachhochschulen*/hautes écoles spécialisées. The already well-developed, but scattered non-university sector which encompassed until now institutions of different status and levels is being progressively redesigned.

fields of commerce and computer science in Belgium (Flemish Community), France, Japan, New Zealand, the United States and also in Australia and the United Kingdom.

Many countries now have a broader range of institutions and programmes than ever before, accommodating both larger numbers and a wider diversity of interests and abilities. Box 5B gives examples. Although many innovations of this type are too recent to be well established, they represent significant efforts on the part of systems and providers to respond to demand, both individual and social.

An important, often unremarked feature of recent patterns of participation is that many new path-

ways are being created, not so much by the deliberate policies pursued by education authorities, but rather by the choices made by the students themselves. These choices reflect strategies aiming to take advantage of the options best suited to individual interests and need. Examples of such new, "spontaneous" pathways in tertiary education are described in Box 5C.

While growing diversity of supply already reflects a responsiveness to demand, there is a need for many countries to reinforce and extend this response. Firstly, they can encourage providers to facilitate further new means of entry to, exit from and mobility within tertiary education (through, for example, wider use of credit transfer and modules). Secondly, they can

Box 5C
DIVERSIFYING QUALIFICATIONS THROUGH STUDENT CHOICE

Double degrees in Australia. There is growing interest in combined or double degrees acquired at a single university, for which arts and law are a long established precedent. Double degrees now increasingly include elements of business, engineering or teacher education. Such studies usually require five years, as compared to a three-year full-time course for a generalist first degree, or four years' study for an honours degree.

Pathways through tertiary education in France. Successful completion of any first-cycle programme of study permits students to pursue studies in any field. As a result, French students follow a variety of paths to advanced degrees. The proportion of graduates of technical, employment-oriented programmes of the university institutes of technology (IUT) and advanced technician sections of the *lycées* who continue their studies has increased over time; by 1992, almost two-thirds of DUT (*Diplôme Universitaire Technologique*) holders and two-fifths of BTS (*Brevet de Technicien Supérieurs*) holders were continuing studies mostly in second cycle programmes in universities, engineering schools and business schools. These proportions are higher than expected, and they have had some influence on the nature of teaching and learning in the first cycle programmes. A related consequence is that technological and vocational *baccalauréat* holders who are unable to find places in IUT and STS (*Sections de Techniciens Supérieurs*) programmes, pursue tertiary studies in open access university programmes. More than 10 pathways to the specialised diplomas of higher education (DESS - *Diplôme d'Etudes Supérieures Spécialisées*) have been identified. The different choices of pathways imply educational costs per student ranging from 166 500 FF to 376 800 FF, reflecting both differences in the annual per student costs within the different elements of the pathways and differences in the average time actually needed to complete the various elements (including re-taking or extending a year's study).[3]

Multiple degrees in the Netherlands. Dutch students choose between higher professional colleges (HBO) and universities, each providing first degree courses usually requiring four years of study. Following the approval in 1988 of an act which provided HBO graduates with the possibility of obtaining a university degree in reduced time, increasing numbers of students now follow such programmes to obtain the two qualifications. While the statutory status of these abridged university degree programmes has been withdrawn and funding is now time-limited, Dutch research indicates that the interest in "stacking" qualifications may well increase as students and their families see this as a means of keeping options open, of making adjustments in choices and of pursuing academic study as an important activity and experience in its own right.

Seminars and workshops organised by student associations in Portugal. Partly in response to a broadening of employment destinations of graduates, Portuguese students are participating in a range of seminars, workshops and activities covering topics such as job search, work experience and entrepreneurship as well as basic computer skills. Within some universities, the activities are being organised by student associations.

Articulation and credit transfer in the United States. Young and adult students follow course modules in community colleges which afford them flexible options for transfer to institutions offering bachelor's degree programmes. In Virginia, a state policy on transfer has defined a "transfer module" which, if successfully completed at a community college, guarantees admission into a bachelor's degree programme in a public institution. One public university has a well-established articulation arrangement with its region's community college; the result is that the university's transfer enrolments are greater than freshman enrolments.

establish broad frameworks that help make alternative pathways and options more feasible. Such frameworks need to be inclusive: specific agreements between institutions on matters such as certification should not foreclose wider regional or system-wide arrangements, providing for quality assurance, standards, assessment and recognition.

---

3.   See CEREQ (1995) and Observatoire des coûts des établissements de l'enseignement supérieur (1997).

5.6 DROP-OUT AND NON-COMPLETION

Concern about failure, drop-out and non-completion has increased with growth and diversity in participation. Social and economic developments call for a shift in the orientation in the first years of tertiary education from selection to inclusiveness. From this perspective, drop-out and failure can be seen as indicators of how well tertiary education is adapted to the interests and backgrounds of learners. A more specific concern relates to the direct financial costs of failure and drop-out. In Belgium (Flemish Community), it is estimated that a 60 per cent improvement in pass rates on end-of-year examinations would reduce the average time to degree completion in universities by about one-fifth of a year in relation to study programmes of 4 to 5 years (longer for physicians).

Estimated rates of non-completion vary widely: 6-13 per cent in the United Kingdom; 23 per cent in Denmark; 29-31 per cent in Germany; and 64 per cent in Italy. Japan is located at the low end of this range, the United States somewhere in the middle.

These figures fail to convey fully the context for and experiences of those identified as "drop-outs" or "non-completers". In Italy, for example, it is estimated that many of the 23 per cent who leave tertiary education early in the course of their studies (accounting for more than a third of the overall rate of non-completion) do so without having attended a lecture or sat an examination (Moortgat, 1996). In the United States, it is increasingly common for learners to register for modular courses with no intention of completing a degree or diploma programme.

More detailed patterns of failure and non-completion for six European cases are presented in Figure 5.7.

Figure 5.7
Non-completion rates
Various forms of failure or non-completion in tertiary education in selected countries, various years

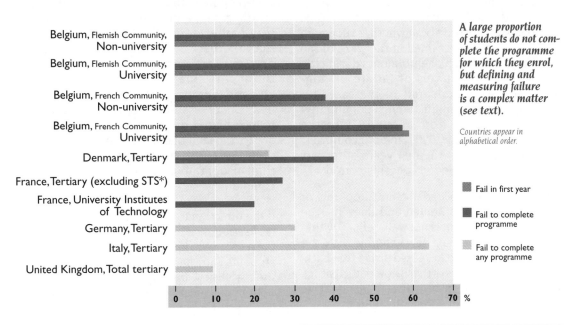

A *large proportion of students do not complete the programme for which they enrol, but defining and measuring failure is a complex matter (see text).*

Countries appear in alphabetical order.

■ Fail in first year

■ Fail to complete programme

▨ Fail to complete any programme

* *Sections de Techniciens Supérieurs.*
Note: Figures have been drawn from several sources, and are therefore subject to differences in coverage and methodology. Further work to improve the comparative information base is needed.
Sources, data and notes for Figure 5.7: page 118.

In interpreting the findings, it should be noted that:

- It is possible to fail in part of the system and still gain a qualification. In Belgium, open access to tertiary education focuses attention on pass rates at the end of the first year, estimated to be about half of all first-time students. But as students may retake failed exams, the proportion who, once enrolled, fail to complete the first cycle of their study programmes is generally lower.

- Changing courses is not the same as dropping out. The available data are weak, but it is estimated that in Denmark for example, while two-fifths of those commencing a course leading to the first degree will fail to complete that programme, 15 per cent will change programmes and institutions. Thus, about one-quarter of those entering tertiary education will leave without acquiring a qualification.

- Non-completion can potentially increase with expansion. In the United Kingdom, although rates of retention and programme completion remain high relative to experience in other countries, concern is being expressed about whether such high rates can be sustained in the wake of the rapid expansion of enrolments during the early 1990s. Rates of failure or non-completion appeared to increase, for example, in Belgium (French Community) and Germany, from about 1970 to the beginning of the 1990s. In both countries, participation in the first years of tertiary education expanded over this period.

Information to help understand "drop-out" or "non-completion" is limited and uneven. The nature of the problem is not well-defined within countries and it may be changing with the growing numbers and increased diversity in backgrounds and interests of those now participating. Non-completion is not always a negative phenomenon. It can potentially reflect:

- an intent to "stop-out", rather than "drop-out".

- a desire by the student merely to take a course rather than a full degree or diploma; or

- a decision to change orientation once enrolled.

On the other hand, non-completion can indicate:

- a failure to realise an intended degree or diploma objective; or

- a lack of an appropriate diversity in options, pathways or range of forms of teaching responsive to the varied backgrounds and interests of learners.

So implications for policy are unclear. Patterns of failure, drop-out and non-completion vary within countries by programme, secondary school qualification, social background and age. The underlying problems giving rise to these patterns have not been fully identified. In France and Belgium (Flemish Community), for example, students with technical and professional preparation in secondary education are more likely to fail in university studies and less likely to fail in short-cycle, non-university programmes. In the United States, studies have demonstrated that the least well-prepared students (as measured by high school grades and scores on college entrance tests) are five times more likely to drop-out than the best-prepared students. Rates of drop-out vary among programmes and institutions, in line with prior preparation of students enrolled. Programmes with larger numbers of less well-prepared students tend to have higher drop-out rates – but this is not always the fault of the programmes, which may do a better job in retaining these students than programmes in which they are less common.

If the direction for development is the gradual realisation of a lifelong approach to learning, the response to failure should not be to channel students into narrow options thought to suit their abilities, but rather to give them more options and greater support. In particular, there is a need for counselling and for instruction methods well suited to students who have followed non-traditional routes, who are older or who come from less well-represented backgrounds.

5.7 CONCLUSIONS

To help shape an appropriate response to wider participation in tertiary education, policy makers need to address the many new interests and needs of a larger student body that is more varied than previously in age, social background and prior educational experience. International indicators that can reflect this diversity do not yet exist. The principal weakness is a lack of comparative information on individual characteristics and choices. Most of the available indicators derive from programme- or institution-reported data, and so fail to provide the kind of information needed to understand better deliberate choices such as programme changes, drop-out/stop-out and combinations of different types of tertiary-level studies.

Policy frameworks in Australia, New Zealand, the United Kingdom and Japan, among others, are seeking to recognise if not foster such choices. With demand, both individual and social, as the driving force, a new orientation is needed in policies and practices of inclusiveness rather than selection. Demand will need to be accommodated with appropriate, effective provision designed at the system, institution and programme levels, and aimed at encouraging participation and reducing failures. Current practices and new initiatives in Member countries are beginning to reflect such an orientation, but more could be and should be done.

Among the key policy implications that follow from this analysis are the following tasks for governments and tertiary education systems:

- to improve quality and to ensure that all young people successfully master core learning objectives through secondary education;

- to promote and sustain diversity in provision, in ways that affect programme content, teaching and learning within as well as among institutions;

- to break from a channelling of students along preset routes, by creating greater flexibility in student pathways in practice as well as policy, and reducing the need to "double-back" when moving from one programme to another;

- to permit learners to time participation in the first years of tertiary education when it is best suited to their capacities, interests and needs;

- to balance this greater flexibility with good information, guidance and structured programmes, teaching and learning to ensure that learning efforts are not wasted;

- to strengthen management and leadership capacities at the institutional level, in order to widen the scope for the exercise of autonomy by providers within a policy framework that encourages responsiveness to demand and supports the development of administrative and teaching staff. ■

References

BLACK, P. and **ATKIN, J.M.** (1996), *Changing the Subject: Innovations in Science, Mathematics and Technology Education*, OECD and Routledge, Paris and London.

CENTRE D'ÉTUDES ET DE RECHERCHES SUR LES QUALIFICATIONS (CEREQ) (1995), "L'insertion professionnelle des diplômés de l'enseignement supérieur se dégrade", *Céreq B'ref* No. 107, Paris, March.

HANSEN, E. J. (1996), *The First Generation of the Welfare State: A Cohort Analysis*, Danish National Institute of Social Research, Copenhagen.

KANE, T.J. (1995), "Rising public college tuition and college entry: How well do public subsidies promote access to college?", National Bureau of Economic Research, *Working Paper No.* 5164, Cambridge, MA.

MOORTGAT, J-L. (1996), *A Study of Dropout in European Higher Education*, Council of Europe, Strasbourg.

MORTENSON, T.G. (1996), "Chance for college by age 19 by state in 1994", *Postsecondary Education Opportunity*, No. 49, The Mortenson Research Seminar on Public Policy Analysis of Opportunity for Postsecondary Education, Iowa City, Iowa.

KANEKO, M. and **KITAMURA, K.** (1995), "Towards mass higher education: Access and participation", Country Case Study - Japan, Mimeo, Ministry of Education, Science and Culture, Tokyo.

OBSERVATOIRE DES COÛTS DES ÉTABLISSEMENTS DE L'ENSEIGNEMENT SUPÉRIEUR (1997), *Les DESS scientifiques: Les parcours diplômants et leurs coûts - résultats de l'enquête sur les diplômes* 1994, Presse universitaire de Grenoble.

OECD (1994), *The OECD Jobs Study*, Paris.

OECD (1996a), *Lifelong Learning for All*, Paris.

OECD (1996b), *Education at a Glance: Analysis*, Paris.

OECD (1997a), *Education and Equity in OECD Countries*, Paris.

OECD (1997b), "Thematic review of the first years of tertiary education", Mimeo, Paris.

OECD (1997c), *Education at a Glance: OECD Indicators*, Paris.

STATISTICAL ANNEX

Data for the figures

Chapter 1

Data for Figure 1.1
GDP per capita (US Dollars), expenditures per student and expenditures per student as a percentage of GDP per capita, 1994

	GDP per capita	Expenditures on educational institutions per student	Expenditures on educational institutions per student as a percentage of GDP per capita	Total expenditures on educational institutions as a percentage of GDP
Australia	18 516	4 690	25.3	5.7
Austria[1]	20 206	6 890	34.1	5.6
Belgium[2,3]	20 316	4 690	23.1	5.5
Canada	20 298	6 640	32.7	7.2
Czech Republic[1,3]	8 883	2 650	29.8	5.7
Denmark	20 445	6 070	29.7	7.0
Finland	16 273	4 820	29.6	6.6
France	19 233	4 700	24.4	6.2
Germany[1]	19 668	5 850	29.7	5.8
Greece[2]	11 590	1 540	13.3	2.4
Hungary[1]	6 302	1 900	30.1	6.4
Ireland	15 783	3 240	20.5	5.7
Italy[1]	18 648	5 030	27.0	4.7
Japan	21 170	5 070	23.9	4.9
Korea	10 405	2 580	24.8	6.2
Mexico	7 822	1 560	19.9	5.6
Netherlands	18 724	4 160	22.2	4.9
New Zealand[3]	15 959	4 100	25.7	5.6
Norway[1,3]	21 954	6 380	29.1	5.7
Spain	13 596	3 170	23.3	5.6
Sweden	17 582	5 680	32.3	6.7
Switzerland[1,3]	23 859	7 110	29.8	5.5
Turkey[1]	5 271	880	16.7	3.4
United Kingdom[2,3]	17 622	4 340	24.6	4.6
United States	25 512	7 790	30.5	6.6
Average of above	*16 625*	*4 461*	*26.1*	*5.6*

1. Public institutions.
2. Public and government-dependent private institutions.
3. Excluding private payments to educational institutions.
Source: OECD Education Database.

Data for Figure 1.2
Youth population aged 5-29 as a percentage of the total population,1995

	Youth population share
Australia	37.2
Austria	33.4
Belgium	32.3
Canada	35.2
Czech Republic	36.2
Denmark	32.1
Finland	32.0
France	34.7
Germany	31.1
Greece	34.7
Hungary	34.8
Iceland	39.3
Ireland	41.8
Italy	32.6
Japan	33.5
Korea	44.7
Mexico	54.1
Netherlands	33.8
New Zealand	37.7
Norway	34.1
Portugal	36.4
Spain	36.8
Sweden	31.7
Switzerland	31.8
Turkey	50.6
United Kingdom	34.7
United States	35.6
Average of above	*36.4*
Average excluding five countries [1]	*34.2*

1. Iceland, Ireland, Korea, Mexico and Turkey.
Source: OECD Education Database.

Data for Figure 1.3a
Net enrolment rates at age 3 and 5, 1995

	Age 3	Age 5
Australia	18.3	92.1
Austria	30.4	90.2
Belgium	98.5	99.7
Canada	-	96.8
Czech Republic	62.8	92.7
Denmark	60.0	82.3
Finland	26.9	35.0
France	99.5	101.7
Germany	46.6	79.2
Greece	12.7	79.4
Hungary	66.0	97.3
Iceland	77.5	-
Ireland	0.9	98.2
Japan	57.6	99.0
Korea	10.4	42.2
Mexico	10.4	80.7
Netherlands	-	99.2
New Zealand	83.3	105.5
Norway	54.5	71.5
Portugal	40.4	64.6
Spain	57.4	103.7
Sweden	51.0	63.4
Switzerland	5.9	79.0
Turkey	0.3	14.3
United Kingdom	44.8	99.8
United States	34.2	100
Average of above	*42.0*	*82.7*

-: missing, not available, not applicable or negligible value.
Source: OECD Education Database.

Data for Figure 1.3b
Net enrolment rates at age 17 and 20, 1995

	Age 17	Age 20
Australia	93.5	46.7
Austria	87.7	25.8
Belgium	100.1	66.7
Canada	79.1	56.7
Czech Republic	71.7	20.3
Denmark	81.7	42.4
Finland	90.5	42.9
France	92.6	55.7
Germany	93.6	45.2
Greece	55.8	36.3
Hungary	71.1	25.0
Iceland	77.4	43.1
Ireland	80.9	37.3
Japan	94.4	-
Korea	89.6	36.4
Luxembourg*	77.7	-
Mexico	37.0	13.6
Netherlands	93.3	59.6
New Zealand	76.8	44.5
Norway	90.3	43.0
Portugal	72.8	44.1
Spain	74.8	49.7
Sweden	95.8	30.6
Switzerland	83.5	33.9
Turkey	25.7	12.1
United Kingdom	74.7	39.2
United States	78.6	35.4
Average of above	*79.3*	*39.4*

-: missing, not available, not applicable or negligible value.
* Net enrolment rates by single year of age are underestimated since they only include those students who attend a public or publicly funded school in Luxembourg. Students who are residents of Luxembourg but attend either a not publicly funded school in Luxembourg or a school in a neighbouring country are *excluded*.
Source: OECD Education Database.

Data for Figure 1.4
Contribution of the youth population and of enrolment rates to higher or lower education expenditures as a percentage of GDP, relative to the OECD average, 1995

	Effect of enrolment rate	Effect of size of youth population (2-29)
Australia	0.01	0.18
Austria[1]	-0.26	-0.63
Belgium[2]	0.91	-0.68
Canada	0.01	-0.19
Czech Republic[1]	-0.11	-0.05
Denmark	0.76	-0.84
Finland	0.61	-0.82
France	0.86	-0.29
Germany[1]	0.16	-1.05
Greece[2]	-0.71	-0.41
Hungary[1]	-0.24	-0.32
Ireland	0.32	0.73
Italy[1]	-0.20	-0.70
Japan	0.07	-0.54
Korea	-0.71	1.10
Mexico	-1.10	1.98
Netherlands	0.24	-0.35
New Zealand	0.22	0.35
Norway[1]	0.61	-0.37
Spain	0.37	-0.09
Sweden	0.23	-0.84
Switzerland[1]	-0.36	-0.77
Turkey[1]	-1.54	0.79
United Kingdom	-0.21	-0.21
United States	-0.05	-0.03
Average of above	*0.00*	*0.16*

1. Public institutions.
2. Public and government-dependent private institutions.
Source: OECD Education Database.

Data for Figure 1.5
Trends in the youth population share, enrolment, and education expenditures, selected countries, 1975-1994

		Enrolment rate (ages 5-29)	Education expenditures relative to GDP (all levels)	Youth population share (ages 5-29)
Austria	1975	100.0	100.0	100.0
	1980	100.0	100.0	99.9
	1985	92.3	101.8	97.1
	1990	92.5	94.7	92.9
	1994	94.7	94.7	89.0
Ireland	1975	100.0	100.0	100.0
	1980	97.8	98.5	102.6
	1985	102.5	92.3	101.9
	1990	109.4	76.9	99.0
	1994	104.3	84.6	97.8
Italy	1975	100.0	100.0	100.0
	1980	100.0	93.8	99.7
	1985	95.3	104.2	99.4
	1990	96.3	108.3	94.7
	1994	99.0	100.0	88.1
Switzerland	1975	100.0	100.0	100.0
	1980	103.9	98.1	95.5
	1985	119.9	96.2	90.7
	1990	116.5	98.1	87.8
	1994	121.4	107.5	81.5

Source: OECD Education Database.

Data for Figure 1.6
Effects of various components on teachers' statutory salary costs[1] per student,[2] relative to the country average, 1995

	Country average, statutory salary cost per student	Level of statutory salary (after 15 years of experience)	Instruction supplied per teacher (hours)	Total teaching time (hours)	Residual	Country statutory salary cost per student enrolled
	Effects on student costs					
	(incremental or decremental effect of specified factor, in US Dollars per student, converted using purchasing power parities)					
	A	B	C	D	E	A+B+C+D+E
	US $	US $	US $	US $	US $	US $
Austria	2 184	-110	+283	+538	+28	2 922
Belgium	2 184	+158	+4	+1 500	-13	3 832
Czech Republic	2 184	-1 569	+46	-90	-47	524
Denmark	2 184	+192	-125	+794	+39	3 083
France	2 184	+78	+181	-379	+89	2 152
Germany	2 184	+624	+28	-741	+247	2 342
Greece	2 184	-810	+260	-474	+75	1 235
Ireland	2 184	+411	-41	-636	+174	2 091
Italy	2 184	-381	+351	+65	+107	2 326
Netherlands	2 184	+482	-677	-103	+205	2 091
New Zealand	2 184	-239	-252	-327	-143	1 224
Norway	2 184	-645	+342	+199	+167	2 246
Portugal	2 184	-202	+104	-247	+50	1 889
Spain	2 184	+50	-423	-141	+33	1 702
Sweden	2 184	-562	+333	-430	+133	1 658
Switzerland	2 184	+1 887	-1 906	+1 271	+662	4 098
United States	2 184	+183	-576	-166	+80	1 706
Average of above		*-27*	*-122*	*+37*	*+111*	*2 184*

1. Teachers with 15 years of experience.
2. Lower secondary level.
Source: OECD Education Database.

Chapter 2

Data for Figure 2.1a
Percentage of women aged 30-44 in employment, by level of educational attainment, 1995

| | Educational attainment | | | | |
	Below upper secondary	Upper secondary	Non-university tertiary	University education	Total
Australia	60	66	76	83	66
Austria	63	75	89	88	73
Belgium	48	70	87	83	66
Canada	51	70	77	82	71
Czech Republic	78	89	-	95	87
Denmark	69	84	91	93	79
Finland	62	73	82	86	73
France	53	71	84	79	69
Germany	56	70	83	82	69
Greece	44	51	73	86	54
Ireland	31	55	75	81	50
Italy	38	66	-	81	52
Korea	67	49	-	49	56
Luxembourg	48	69	-	79	55
Netherlands	47	66	-	81	63
New Zealand	60	69	74	77	67
Norway	59	79	84	90	79
Poland	59	70	86	92	72
Portugal	67	80	94	95	73
Spain	33	51	55	77	43
Sweden	70	83	90	89	83
Switzerland	69	69	73	78	70
Turkey	31	33	-	67	33
United Kingdom	51	70	84	84	69
United States	49	72	82	81	73
Average of above	*55*	*68*	*81*	*82*	*66*

- : missing value, or category not applicable.
Sources: Labour force survey or equivalent data for 1995 or latest year; and OECD Education Database.

Data for Figure 2.1b
Unemployment rates, ages 30-44, by level of educational attainment, 1995

| | Educational attainment | | | | |
	Below upper secondary	Upper secondary	Non-university tertiary	University education	Total
Australia	8.8	5.9	4.9	3.2	6.5
Austria	5.7	2.4	0.9	2.2	3.1
Belgium	15.1	7.5	3.6	3.6	9.0
Canada	14.6	8.7	7.4	5.0	8.5
Czech Republic	8.7	2.1	-	0.8	2.7
Denmark	13.2	6.6	4.2	3.7	8.6
Finland	21.6	15.3	8.8	5.6	14.7
France	17.1	9.4	4.8	6.4	10.1
Germany	13.0	7.3	4.5	4.6	7.4
Greece	7.5	7.6	7.3	4.7	7.0
Ireland	18.6	7.6	4.5	3.0	11.1
Italy	10.0	6.3	-	5.9	8.1
Korea	1.2	1.4	-	1.4	1.3
Luxembourg	3.9	2.4	-	0.7	3.1
Netherlands	9.8	5.2	-	3.7	6.1
New Zealand	7.4	3.3	4.0	3.2	4.8
Norway	8.6	4.0	3.6	1.7	3.9
Poland	19.4	11.6	6.2	2.0	11.5
Portugal	7.0	5.3	2.5	1.8	6.0
Spain	22.8	16.8	13.7	10.4	19.0
Sweden	12.3	9.2	5.1	4.5	8.3
Switzerland	6.0	2.6	1.7	2.7	3.0
Turkey	4.3	4.4	-	2.1	4.1
United Kingdom	15.2	7.1	3.6	3.0	7.2
United States	11.3	5.3	3.6	2.2	4.8
Average of above	*11.3*	*6.6*	*5.0*	*3.5*	*7.2*

- : missing value, or category not applicable.
Sources: Labour force survey or equivalent data for 1995 or latest year; and OECD Education Database.

Data for Figure 2.2
Relative mean earnings of women and men aged 30-44, by level of educational attainment, 1995:
Earnings for those with upper secondary education only = 100

	Women			Men		
	Below upper secondary education	Non-university tertiary education	University education	Below upper secondary education	Non-university tertiary education	University education
Australia	86	102	144	101	118	163
Canada	-	114	167	82	110	150
Czech Republic	77	-	154	71	-	154
Denmark	86	108	129	87	107	138
Finland	91	123	169	89	121	175
France	73	139	170	86	138	180
Germany	88	114	165	90	105	148
Ireland *	61	123	197	78	122	169
Italy	76	-	120	79	-	139
Netherlands	71	134	160	83	121	148
New Zealand	84	108	146	82	102	163
Norway	80	131	147	81	129	153
Portugal	63	-	174	62	-	176
Sweden	86	111	138	88	119	152
Switzerland	76	145	161	74	122	132
United Kingdom	76	159	210	77	115	162
United States	59	127	186	63	120	170
Average of above	*77*	*124*	*161*	*81*	*118*	*157*

- : missing value, or category not applicable.
* Data refer to 1994.
Source: OECD Education Database.

Data for Figure 2.3
Estimated rates of return to university and upper secondary education, over a working lifetime,
for women and men, 1995

	Women			Men		
	Upper secondary education	Non-university tertiary education	University education	Upper secondary education	Non-university tertiary education	University education
Australia	12.5	7.9	6.7	7.5	9.7	10.4
Canada	16.1	28.1	28.5	12.5	23.0	16.5
Czech Republic	13.8	-	7.0	22.0	-	8.7
Denmark	11.8	5.1	9.2	10.4	5.2	11.0
Finland	8.1	12.2	14.3	10.4	10.5	14.8
France	14.1	20.1	12.7	14.2	17.6	14.1
Germany	5.5	8.7	8.2	5.7	16.6	10.9
Ireland *	28.8	8.2	17.4	18.6	11.7	14.0
Italy	9.5	-	4.6	10.4	-	9.9
Netherlands	24.4	-	10.5	14.1	-	10.8
New Zealand	11.2	-0.5	10.3	12.8	-11.5	11.6
Norway	17.3	7.8	13.3	11.3	9.4	11.6
Sweden	9.9	4.2	5.3	10.9	6.5	8.2
Switzerland	22.1	17.7	5.2	19.0	27.1	5.5
United Kingdom	19.1	13.7	19.1	14.3	4.8	12.7
United States	22.9	10.5	12.6	26.3	8.9	12.6
Average of above	*15.4*	*11.1*	*11.6*	*13.8*	*10.7*	*11.5*

- : missing value, or category not applicable.
* Data refer to 1994.
Source: OECD Education Database.

Data for Figure 2.4a
Percentage of population aged 25-64 having completed upper secondary education, assuming 1995 youth qualification rates

	Percentage with upper secondary education or higher			Rank order		
	1995	2005	2015	1995	2005	2015
Australia	53	58	62	15	15	17
Austria	69	76	79	8	9	10
Belgium	53	64	70	14	14	12
Canada	75	81	84	6	7	7
Denmark	62	66	69	11	11	13
Finland	65	74	81	10	10	9
France	68	79	84	9	8	8
Germany	84	88	89	2	2	1
Greece	43	57	66	17	17	16
Ireland	47	58	66	16	16	15
Italy	35	48	57	18	18	18
Netherlands	61	66	70	12	12	11
New Zealand	59	64	68	13	13	14
Norway	81	86	89	4	4	2
Portugal	20	30	36	20	20	20
Spain	28	41	49	19	19	19
Sweden	75	82	87	7	6	5
Switzerland	82	86	88	3	3	4
United Kingdom	76	82	86	5	5	6
United States	86	88	88	1	1	3
Average of above	*61*	*69*	*73*			

Notes: • The methodology used in the calculations applies existing or assumed levels of educational attainment by 5-year age-groups in the adult population (25-64 years of age) to the projected numbers in the total population by age-group for each year between 1995 and 2015. Thus, the level of educational attainment currently reached by the "youth population", defined as the 25-29 age-group, spreads to the older age-groups over time.
• The calculations are based on the assumption that youth qualification rates will remain at the 1995 level.
See also notes to Figure 2.4b.
Sources: UN Population Database and UN World Population Prospects (1950-2050); and OECD Education Database.

Data for Figure 2.4b
Proportion of population aged 25-29 required to have completed upper secondary education, for overall adult educational attainment to reach a specified threshold by 2015

	Adult population — Percentage of population aged 25-64 with at least upper secondary education			Youth population — Percentage of 25-29 year-olds with at least upper secondary education	
	A — Current situation (1995)	B — 2015 situation (corresponding to col. D)	C — Threshold in year 2015 (corresponding to col. E)	D — Actual situation (1995)	E — Required in order to reach threshold
Australia	53	62	75	58	93
Austria	69	79	85	81	94
Belgium	53	70	75	74	88
Canada	75	84	88	85	94
Denmark	62	69	75	70	84
Finland	65	81	85	82	93
France	68	84	85	87	90
Germany	84	89	90	89	92
Greece	43	66	70	68	83
Ireland	47	66	70	67	80
Italy	35	57	60	51	77
Netherlands	61	70	75	72	84
New Zealand	59	68	75	64	85
Norway	81	89	90	89	93
Portugal	20	36	50	35	72
Spain	28	49	60	51	80
Sweden	75	87	88	90	92
Switzerland	82	88	90	91	94
United Kingdom	76	86	88	87	93
United States	86	88	90	87	92
Average of above	*61*	*73*	*78*	*74*	*88*

Notes: • The data show the implications of a closing of the gap in educational attainment of the adult population over a 20-year period. To achieve a given level of attainment in the adult population in 2015 (for example, 85 per cent in Austria at upper secondary or higher levels, compared to 69 per cent in 1995, it would be necessary for Austria to achieve a level of attainment equivalent to 94 per cent for the 25-29 age-group in each year between 1996 and 2015).
• Column A shows the level of educational attainment of the adult population in 1995.
• Column B shows the projected attainment level of the adult population in 2015 on the assumption of no change in the level of educational attainment of the youth population observed in 1995 (shown in Column D). In other words, if the overall attainment of the 20-24 or 30-34 age-group is higher than that of the 25-29 age-group in 1995, the highest value in 1995 is applied to each cohort of 25-29 year-olds in years following 1995.
• Column C shows a set of threshold attainment levels for the adult population in 2015 based on some "catching-up" by low attainment countries in the period from 1995 to 2015. Different levels of educational attainment in the adult population are assumed to have been reached by the year 2015: 90 per cent for those countries which were above 86 per cent in 1995; 88 per cent for those which were close to 75 per cent in 1995; 85 per cent for those in the 65-69 per cent bracket, and so on.
• The levels of youth educational attainment, for young adults aged 25-29, required to reach the specified threshold levels by 2015 are shown in Column E. The values shown may not necessarily be close to current or likely graduation rates from upper secondary or tertiary education because the attainment levels of the 25-29 age-group tend to reflect the rate of graduation over the previous 10-15 years – a period during which some countries accelerated their graduation rates. To some extent, the possibility that a rapid acceleration has occurred in graduation rates in recent years has been taken into account by insuring that projected attainment levels of the 25-29 age-group are at least as high as that of the 20-24 age-group in 1995 if the latter exceeds that of the 25-29 age-group.
• The projected level of educational attainment of the age-group 30-45 may have been underestimated for countries in which a significant group of people graduate from tertiary-level institutions at an age above 29. Furthermore, the projections do not take into account the possibility that lifelong learning may progressively become a reality for a majority of people, and that many adults beyond 29 may obtain new and higher qualifications.
Sources: UN Population Database and UN World Population Prospects (1950-2050); and OECD Education Database.

Data for Figure 2.5
Percentage of population aged 26-65 who participate in education or training, classified by source of funding, and main programme undertaken, 1994

		(a) Main programme undertaken			(b) Source of funding for job-related programmes		
		Formal	Informal	Total	Employer	Other	Total
Canada	Job-related	24	4	28	17	11	28
	Other training	7	2	9			
Netherlands	Job-related	17	5	22	15	7	22
	Other training	9	5	14			
Poland	Job-related	10	1	11	7	4	11
	Other training	3	1	4			
Switzerland (French-speaking)	Job-related	16	3	19	11	8	19
	Other training	10	5	15			
Switzerland (German-speaking)	Job-related	21	3	24	14	10	24
	Other training	13	9	22			
United States	Job-related	31	5	36	26	10	36
	Other training	4	4	8			
Average of above	*Job-related*	*20*	*4*	*23*	*15*	*8*	*23*
	Other training	*8*	*4*	*12*			

Note: The distinction between participation in different types of training is made on the basis of the *main* training programme taken by individuals during the 12 months preceding the interview.

Definitions applied

Education and training refers to all courses (including recreation), workshops, on-the-job training, and apprenticeship training undertaken by individuals during the 12 months prior to the survey conducted in 1994.

Informal education or training includes learning that:
• does not relate to programmes leading to a qualification;
• is not related to programmes organised by a formal educational institution;
• is undertaken either in a work or home environment; and
• is not related to classroom instruction, seminars or workshops.

Formal education or training relates to all other types of organised learning, including:
• all education or training taking place in institutions such as schools, colleges, training centres and community centres; and
• all education or training leading to a qualification.

Job-related training refers to all courses undertaken for career or job-related purposes as distinct from personal or other interests.
Employer-sponsored training refers to training which was financed at least to some extent by employers even if other sources of funding were used in combination.
Other funding refers to education or training which was funded by government, self or others, but not by employers.

Source: OECD and Statistics Canada, International Adult Literacy Survey.

Chapter 3

Data for Figure 3.1
Proportion of population aged 16-65 who are at a particular literacy level, relative to the Level 3 baseline, 1994-1995

A. Prose scale

	Level 1		Level 2		Level 3		Level 4/5	
Australia	-17.0	(0.6)	-27.1	(0.6)	36.9	(0.5)	18.9	(0.4)
Belgium (Flanders)	-18.4	(1.5)	-28.2	(2.1)	39.0	(2.4)	14.3	(1.2)
Canada	-16.6	(1.6)	-25.6	(1.8)	35.1	(2.4)	22.7	(2.3)
Germany	-14.4	(0.9)	-34.2	(1.0)	38.0	(1.3)	13.4	(1.0)
Ireland	-22.6	(1.4)	-29.8	(1.6)	34.1	(1.2)	13.5	(1.4)
Netherlands	-10.5	(0.6)	-30.1	(0.9)	44.1	(1.0)	15.3	(0.6)
New Zealand	-18.4	(0.9)	-27.3	(1.0)	35.0	(0.8)	19.2	(0.7)
Poland	-42.6	(0.9)	-34.5	(0.9)	19.8	(0.7)	3.1	(0.3)
Sweden	-7.5	(0.5)	-20.3	(0.6)	39.7	(0.9)	32.4	(0.5)
Switzerland (French-speaking)	-17.6	(1.3)	-33.7	(1.6)	38.6	(1.8)	10.0	(0.7)
Switzerland (German-speaking)	-19.3	(1.0)	-35.7	(1.6)	36.0	(1.3)	8.9	(1.0)
United Kingdom	-21.8	(1.0)	-30.3	(1.2)	31.3	(1.1)	16.6	(0.7)
United States	-20.7	(0.7)	-25.9	(1.1)	32.4	(1.2)	21.1	(1.2)
Average of above	*-19.0*		*-29.4*		*35.4*		*16.1*	

B. Document scale

	Level 1		Level 2		Level 3		Level 4/5	
Australia	-17.0	(0.5)	-27.8	(0.7)	37.7	(0.7)	17.4	(0.6)
Belgium (Flanders)	-15.3	(1.7)	-24.2	(2.8)	43.2	(4.1)	17.2	(0.9)
Canada	-18.2	(1.9)	-24.7	(1.5)	32.1	(1.8)	25.1	(1.3)
Germany	-9.0	(0.7)	-32.7	(1.2)	39.5	(1.0)	18.9	(1.0)
Ireland	-25.3	(1.7)	-31.7	(1.2)	31.5	(1.3)	11.5	(1.2)
Netherlands	-10.1	(0.7)	-25.7	(0.8)	44.2	(0.9)	20.0	(0.8)
New Zealand	-21.4	(0.9)	-29.2	(1.1)	31.9	(0.8)	17.6	(0.7)
Poland	-45.4	(1.3)	-30.7	(1.0)	18.0	(0.7)	5.8	(0.3)
Sweden	-6.2	(0.4)	-18.9	(0.7)	39.4	(0.8)	35.5	(0.6)
Switzerland (French-speaking)	-16.2	(1.3)	-28.8	(1.4)	38.9	(1.3)	16.0	(1.1)
Switzerland (German-speaking)	-18.1	(1.0)	-29.1	(1.5)	36.7	(0.8)	16.1	(1.0)
United Kingdom	-23.3	(1.0)	-27.1	(1.0)	30.5	(1.0)	19.1	(1.0)
United States	-23.7	(0.8)	-25.9	(1.1)	31.4	(0.9)	19.0	(1.0)
Average of above	*-19.2*		*-27.4*		*35.0*		*18.4*	

C. Quantitative scale

	Level 1		Level 2		Level 3		Level 4/5	
Australia	-16.8	(0.5)	-26.5	(0.6)	37.7	(0.6)	19.1	(0.6)
Belgium (Flanders)	-16.7	(1.8)	-23.0	(1.7)	37.8	(2.0)	22.6	(1.3)
Canada	-16.9	(1.8)	-26.1	(2.5)	34.8	(2.1)	22.2	(1.8)
Germany	-6.7	(0.4)	-26.6	(1.2)	43.2	(0.8)	23.5	(0.9)
Ireland	-24.8	(1.5)	-28.3	(0.8)	30.7	(1.0)	16.2	(1.6)
Netherlands	-10.3	(0.7)	-25.5	(0.9)	44.3	(1.0)	19.9	(0.8)
New Zealand	-20.4	(1.0)	-28.9	(1.1)	33.4	(0.8)	17.2	(0.8)
Poland	-39.1	(1.1)	-30.1	(1.2)	23.9	(0.6)	6.8	(0.5)
Sweden	-6.6	(0.4)	-18.6	(0.6)	39.0	(0.9)	35.8	(0.7)
Switzerland (French-speaking)	-12.9	(0.9)	-24.5	(1.4)	42.2	(1.6)	20.4	(1.0)
Switzerland (German-speaking)	-14.1	(1.0)	-26.2	(1.3)	40.7	(1.4)	19.0	(1.3)
United Kingdom	-23.2	(0.9)	-27.8	(1.0)	30.4	(0.9)	18.6	(1.0)
United States	-21.0	(0.7)	-25.3	(1.1)	31.2	(0.8)	22.5	(1.0)
Average of above	*-17.7*		*-26.0*		*36.1*		*20.3*	

Standard errors of estimates in brackets.
Source: OECD and Statistics Canada, International Adult Literacy Survey.

Data for Figure 3.2
Proportion of employed people aged 25-65 at each literacy level who are in the top 60 per cent of earners: percentage points difference from level 3, 1994-1995

A. Prose scale

	Level I		Level 2		Level 4/5	
Australia	-8.5	(1.5)	-3.1	(1.5)	2.7	(1.8)
Belgium (Flanders)**	-17.1	(2.1)	-5.8	(3.0)	9.6	(3.4)
Canada	-23.9	(7.7)	-8.9	(5.7)	7.0	(1.6)
Germany	-8.0	(6.9)	-5.6	(2.8)	5.9	(2.2)
Ireland	-31.3	(3.0)	-4.5	(2.2)	12.5	(3.5)
Netherlands	-6.3	(7.0)	1.1	(2.3)	-0.7	(3.1)
New Zealand	-9.1	(1.5)	-3.9	(2.0)	6.2	(3.1)
Poland	-13.8	(2.9)	-6.6	(1.6)	14.1	(1.0)
Sweden	-0.3	(3.0)	-1.2*	(3.6)	1.0	(3.3)
Switzerland (French-speaking)	-13.6	(7.6)	-6.7	(3.7)	-7.1*	(5.6)
Switzerland (German-speaking)	-17.1	(4.6)	-9.3	(3.6)	-0.3*	(5.0)
United Kingdom	-21.1	(1.8)	-9.7	(1.6)	10.2	(2.7)
United States	-38.5	(2.1)	-17.9	(3.1)	8.5	(3.4)
Average of above	*-16.0*		*-6.3*		*5.4*	

B. Quantitative scale

	Level I		Level 2		Level 4/5	
Australia	-15.3	(1.6)	-5.6	(1.6)	10.9	(1.6)
Belgium (Flanders)**	-18.9	(2.5)	-1.6	(1.6)	13.6	(3.6)
Canada	-24.8	(4.7)	-12.5	(8.7)	10.4	(3.2)
Germany	-10.4*	(6.3)	-5.6	(5.3)	6.9	(2.0)
Ireland	-29.3	(4.1)	-10.8	(2.9)	9.7	(2.9)
Netherlands	-16.0	(6.2)	-3.6	(3.0)	5.7	(2.5)
New Zealand	-17.2	(1.7)	-5.8	(1.6)	5.7	(2.5)
Poland	-11.7	(2.5)	-3.4	(2.5)	15.1	(0.9)
Sweden	-18.5	(1.8)	-2.7	(3.8)	0.1	(2.0)
Switzerland (French-speaking)	-14.6*	(11.0)	-2.8	(5.3)	5.6*	(4.1)
Switzerland (German-speaking)	-21.4*	(6.6)	-19.1	(3.6)	2.3*	(3.2)
United Kingdom	-25.5	(1.9)	-10.0	(2.2)	17.1	(2.2)
United States	-38.2	(2.9)	-18.3	(2.6)	16.2	(2.4)
Average of above	*-20.1*		*-7.8*		*9.2*	

Standard errors of estimates in brackets. Standard errors are for the percentage at the level.
* Unreliable estimate, due to non-response or low cell count.
** Categories used in the background questionnaire for collecting earnings data do not allow the respondents to be classified in groups of equal size. Data are therefore not shown in Figure 3.2.
Source: OECD and Statistics Canada, International Adult Literacy Survey.

Data for Figure 3.3
Mean score on quantitative scale with range of 0-500 points of adults aged 25-65 by highest completed level of education, 1994-1995

	Educational attainment									
	Primary education or less		Lower secondary education		Upper secondary education		Non-university tertiary education		University education	
Australia	164.3	(4.6)	258.9	(1.7)	282.0	(2.5)	297.7	(1.7)	323.0	(2.0)
Belgium (Flanders)	219.8	(6.1)	268.1	(3.4)	285.7	(3.0)	315.7	(2.5)	334.5	(4.0)
Canada	188.7	(8.9)	254.3	(5.0)	286.2	(4.9)	301.1	(4.8)	344.5	(12.3)
Germany	250.3	(12.6)*	285.3	(1.8)	295.7	(2.9)	306.7	(3.0)	323.2	(4.3)
Ireland	207.5	(6.0)	256.6	(1.6)	286.5	(4.5)	298.3	(3.5)	325.5	(4.7)
Netherlands	234.8	(3.7)	275.4	(1.5)	299.2	(1.8)	n.a.	n.a.	316.3	(2.1)
New Zealand	178.3	(11.2)	253.1	(2.0)	288.2	(2.7)	295.6	(3.5)	315.6	(4.5)
Poland	179.5	(3.4)	226.3	(2.6)	262.4	(2.3)	274.0	(5.2)	291.5	(4.3)
Sweden	261.1	(3.2)	299.8	(4.3)	306.2	(2.1)	320.5	(3.5)	342.0	(3.9)
Switzerland (French-speaking)	225.1	(9.3)	251.6	(4.3)	291.9	(2.3)	308.2	(4.0)	310.5	(5.7)
Switzerland (German-speaking)	199.8	(12.4)*	244.3	(8.7)	288.5	(2.1)	304.7	(3.5)	308.4	(6.7)
United Kingdom	184.8	(10.2)	251.6	(2.6)	287.7	(3.9)	300.1	(3.1)	327.0	(2.8)
United States	183.2	(6.2)	208.4	(8.8)	274.1	(3.0)	294.7	(3.5)	323.5	(3.0)
Average of above	*205.9*		*256.4*		*287.3*		*301.4*		*322.0*	

n.a.: not applicable.
* Sample size is insufficient to permit a reliable estimate. Standard errors of estimates in brackets.
Source: OECD and Statistics Canada, International Adult Literacy Survey.

Data for Figure 3.4
Participation rates (percentages) of employed persons aged 25-64 in job-related adult education and training over a 12-month period, by educational attainment, selected countries, various years

	Year	Gender	Primary education or less	Lower secondary education	Upper secondary education	Non-university tertiary education	University education	Total, all levels of education
Australia	1995	Men + Women	12	28	36	47	58	38
		Men	17	28	36	46	58	38
		Women	5	28	38	49	58	38
Canada	1993	Men + Women	6	12	25	35	43	28
		Men	6	13	22	36	40	27
		Women	5	11	28	34	47	30
Finland	1995	Men + Women	-	31	44	61	65	45
		Men	-	30	43	63	65	45
		Women	-	31	44	59	63	45
Germany	1994	Men + Women	-	15	28	43	50	33
		Men	-	-	29	44	50	35
		Women	-	14	28	40	50	31
Switzerland	1996	Men + Women	-	13	35	53	48	35
		Men	-	12	35	54	49	38
		Women	-	13	34	51	46	31
Sweden	1996	Men + Women	-	27	37	57	61	42
		Men	-	28	35	56	56	39
		Women	-	27	40	58	67	44
United States	1995	Men + Women	7	13	24	36	49	34
		Men	8	11	21	34	45	31
		Women	6	15	27	38	54	36
Average of above		Men + Women	8	20	33	47	53	36
		Men	10	20	32	48	52	36
		Women	5	20	34	47	55	36

-: missing value, or included in another category.
Source: OECD Education Database.

Data for Figure 3.5
Percentage of skilled craft workers who perform[1] particular reading tasks at work at least once a week, 1994-1995

	Average for reading tasks		Letters or memos		Manuals or reference books		Diagrams or schemas	
Australia	56.0	(2.0)	61.3	(2.5)	55.1	(2.2)	71.8	(1.8)
Belgium (Flanders)	26.3	(5.1)	37.2	(4.0)	27.0	(4.1)	31.5	(3.8)
Canada	36.2	(3.3)	43.3	(7.1)	37.5	(7.1)	49.4	(7.8)
Germany	56.2	(5.3)	68.6	(5.4)	61.5	(4.3)	75.1	(5.2)
Ireland	31.6	(5.0)	39.2	(5.9)	39.0	(3.1)	46.0	(4.2)
Netherlands	34.2	(4.2)	38.2	(4.5)	50.7	(3.7)	39.9	(4.1)
New Zealand	57.7	(4.1)	58.0	(4.2)	65.5	(4.7)	80.8	(3.1)
Poland	15.5	(4.3)	16.6	(2.1)	13.4	(1.4)	28.7	(2.2)
Sweden	n.a.		43.5	(3.2)	43.1	(3.4)	34.1	(2.3)
Switzerland (French-speaking)	49.8	(5.1)	54.9	(5.7)	56.3	(4.2)	57.2	(5.4)
Switzerland (German-speaking)	48.5	(5.0)	69.2	(4.0)	63.1	(6.1)	32.4	(7.2)
United Kingdom	44.0	(2.7)	61.2	(3.1)	50.0	(3.4)	57.7	(3.5)
United States	44.7	(4.1)	53.6	(4.0)	54.2	(4.5)	58.4	(5.0)
Average of above	41.7		49.6		47.4		51.0	

n.a.: not applicable.
1. Self-reports of performance.
Source: OECD and Statistics Canada, International Adult Literacy Survey.

Data for Figure 3.6a
Proportion of skilled craft workers and machine operators at each level, document scale, 1994-1995

	Level 1		Level 2		Level 3		Level 4/5	
Australia	20.4	(1.4)	33.6	(1.3)	35.2	(1.6)	10.7	(1.3)
Belgium (Flanders)	18.6	(2.6)	28.8	(3.9)	40.5	(4.0)	12.1	(2.6)
Canada	26.2	(6.3)	30.9	(5.1)	27.6	(5.8)	15.3	(1.6)
Germany	8.1*	(2.6)	37.2	(3.5)	42.6	(3.5)	12.1	(2.5)
Ireland	21.7	(2.6)	35.5	(3.9)	34.8	(3.5)	8.0*	(2.4)
Netherlands	10.5	(1.9)	35.2	(3.0)	38.0	(3.3)	16.3	(2.8)
New Zealand	23.1	(2.9)	35.8	(3.1)	29.9	(2.7)	11.2	(1.7)
Poland	50.6	(1.9)	29.4	(2.1)	15.3	(2.1)	4.7*	(0.9)
Sweden	8.0	(1.3)	18.0	(2.7)	44.8	(4.7)	29.2	(3.3)
Switzerland (French-speaking)	23.0	(3.9)	29.9	(4.2)	30.4	(5.0)	16.7*	(4.0)
Switzerland (German-speaking)	24.2	(3.7)	34.4	(5.3)	32.3	(3.0)	9.1*	(2.4)
United Kingdom	23.2	(2.0)	37.9	(2.3)	28.2	(2.0)	10.7	(1.7)
United States	33.0	(1.9)	34.6	(2.5)	25.4	(2.2)	7.0	(1.3)
Average of above	*22.4*		*32.4*		*32.7*		*12.5*	

Standard error of estimates in brackets.
* Sample size is insufficient to permit a reliable estimate.
Source: OECD and Statistics Canada, International Adult Literacy Survey.

Data for Figure 3.6b
Employed people aged 16-65 who report that their reading, writing and basic mathematical skills are little used at work: proportion who rate their skills as "good" or "excellent", 1994-1995

	Good reading skills		Good writing skills		Good basic mathematics skills	
Australia	86.3	(1.0)	85.1	(0.9)	81.8	(0.9)
Belgium (Flanders)	90.0	(2.7)	82.7	(3.0)	80.0	(3.6)
Canada	81.6	(2.5)	79.7	(2.0)	78.6	(4.4)
Germany	84.8	(3.3)	87.1	(2.7)	88.1	(1.8)
Ireland	83.8	(3.0)	81.9	(2.7)	67.3	(3.1)
Netherlands	74.2	(1.7)	64.8	(2.0)	69.5	(2.1)
New Zealand	85.7	(2.0)	80.3	(1.6)	72.0	(1.9)
Poland	81.1	(0.8)	79.4	(1.3)	71.9	(2.1)
Switzerland (French-speaking)	75.9	(3.4)	65.2	(2.9)	73.3	(2.7)
Switzerland (German-speaking)	84.5	(3.6)	80.2	(2.6)	90.9	(1.6)
United Kingdom	76.7	(2.0)	70.6	(1.3)	64.0	(2.1)
United States	78.1	(2.2)	78.2	(2.0)	82.4	(2.0)
Average of above	*81.9*		*77.9*		*76.7*	

Standard error of estimates in brackets.
Sweden did not ask all of the questions and is therefore excluded from this analysis.
Source: OECD and Statistics Canada, International Adult Literacy Survey.

Data for Figure 3.7a,b,c
Proportion of population aged 16-65 who reported engaging in newspaper reading, television viewing and community activity, 1994-1995

	(a) Reading newspaper		(b) Television viewing		(c) Participating in community activity	
	Daily	Not every day	More than 2 hours a day	2 hours or fewer a day	At least once a month	Less than once a month
Australia	63.4 (0.7)	36.6 (0.7)	*Did not ask question*		25.6 (0.8)	74.4 (0.8)
Belgium (Flanders)	55.4 (2.8)	44.6 (2.8)	37.0 (2.9)	63.0 (2.9)	24.1 (1.0)	75.9 (1.0)
Canada	59.2 (2.7)	40.8 (2.7)	39.2 (2.2)	60.8 (2.2)	23.4 (1.8)	76.6 (1.8)
Germany	82.8 (1.0)	17.2 (1.0)	50.2 (1.6)	49.8 (1.6)	25.6 (0.8)	74.4 (0.8)
Ireland	73.0 (2.6)	27.0 (2.6)	46.2 (1.4)	53.8 (1.4)	28.9 (1.6)	71.1 (1.6)
Netherlands	78.8 (1.0)	21.2 (1.0)	44.9 (1.2)	55.1 (1.2)	31.5 (0.9)	68.5 (0.9)
New Zealand	69.4 (1.1)	30.6 (1.1)	43.9 (1.0)	56.1 (1.0)	32.9 (1.2)	67.1 (1.2)
Poland	61.0 (1.4)	39.0 (1.4)	37.8 (0.8)	62.2 (0.8)	8.9 (0.5)	91.1 (0.5)
Sweden	89.9 (0.6)	10.1 (0.6)	*Did not ask question*		47.2 (0.9)	52.8 (0.9)
Switzerland (French-speaking)	79.0 (1.3)	21.0 (1.3)	27.8 (1.9)	72.2 (1.9)	20.2 (1.4)	79.8 (1.4)
Switzerland (German-speaking)	84.4 (1.2)	15.6 (1.2)	18.7 (1.3)	81.3 (1.3)	23.1 (1.3)	76.9 (1.3)
United Kingdom	71.9 (0.9)	28.1 (0.9)	59.9 (1.0)	40.1 (1.0)	19.2 (0.9)	80.8 (0.9)
United States	63.7 (1.8)	36.3 (1.8)	40.0 (1.4)	60.0 (1.4)	33.5 (1.7)	66.5 (1.7)
Average of above	*71.7*	*28.3*	*40.5*	*59.5*	*26.5*	*73.5*

Standard error of estimates in brackets.
Source: OECD and Statistics Canada, International Adult Literacy Survey.

Chapter 4

Data for Figure 4.1
13-14 year-old students[1] considered as low-achievers[2] in reading (1991), mathematics and science (1994-1995)

	Low scoring students (in percentages) in:			Mean scores by country (in points) in:		
	Reading	**Mathematics**	**Science**	**Reading**	**Mathematics**	**Science**
Australia*	-	(15.9)	(14.7)	-	530	546
Austria*	-	(12.5)	(9.5)	-	540	558
Belgium						
- Flemish Community	-	6.9	8.2	-	565	550
- French Community*	28.4	(14.2)	(33.8)	446	526	471
Canada	-	13.7	14.3	-	528	531
(British Columbia)	17.9	-	-	494	-	-
Czech Republic	-	6.4	4.5	-	564	574
Denmark*	n.a.	(19.7)	(30.4)	n.a.	503	479
Finland	4.7	-	-	545	-	-
France	5.3	6.9	20.0	531	539	498
Germany* [3]	-	(18.6)	(15.8)	-	509	531
- TFGDR	12.3	-	-	501	-	-
- FTFR	16.6	-	-	498	-	-
Greece*	16.1	(28.1)	(22.8)	482	484	497
Hungary	-	12.6	8.4	-	538	554
Iceland	13.1	22.4	21.6	514	487	494
Ireland	20.6	15.2	14.1	484	528	539
Italy	16.4	-	-	488	-	-
Japan	-	4.4	6.5	-	605	571
Korea	-	6.3	8.1	-	607	565
Netherlands*	17.6	(11.9)	(7.0)	486	541	560
New Zealand	15.1	20.0	17.6	528	508	526
Norway	13.6	18.2	13.3	489	503	527
Portugal	7.1	38.2	26.6	500	455	480
Spain	25.1	22.3	13.4	456	487	517
Sweden	10.6	14.8	12.8	529	519	535
Switzerland	10.7	8.8	15.6	515	546	522
United Kingdom - England	-	20.5	13.1	-	507	553
- Scotland*	-	(22.0)	(19.0)	-	500	519
United States	15.5	22.6	16.2	514	500	535
Average of above	*15*	*16*	*15*	*500*	*525*	*529*
Standard deviation				*100*	*95*	*96*

- : The country did not participate in that part of the study. n.a. : not available.
* Countries did not satisfy one or more TIMSS sampling guidelines. Since sampling imperfections may have affected the estimation of the percentage of under-achievers, the values are presented in brackets.
1. Population II, "14-year-olds", for reading; "8th grade" students with a majority of 13-year-olds for mathematics and science. "7th grade" students for Denmark.
2. Students scoring more than one standard deviation below the mean score of the OECD countries who participated in the IEA studies. The international mean for reading was 500 points, for mathematics 525 points and for science 529 points. For most countries, standard errors of the estimates are given in *Education at a Glance: OECD Indicators*, 1994 and 1997 editions.
3. Germany TFGDR refers to the territory of the former Democratic Republic; FTFR refers to the former territory of the Federal Republic.
Sources: IEA, *Reading Literacy Study*; and IEA, *Third International Mathematics and Science Study*.

Data for Figure 4.2
**Ranges of achievement (among 13-14 year-old students[1]) in reading[2] (1991),
and mathematics[3] and science[4] (1994-1995)**
(lower and upper quartiles, relative to international mean, in equivalent years' progress)

	Inter-quartile range (in points) for:			Inter-quartile range (in equivalent year's progress) for:			25th percentile (in points) for:		
	Reading	Mathematics	Science	Reading	Mathematics	Science	Reading	Mathematics	Science
Australia*	-	140	144	-	4.2	3.6	-	460	475
Austria*	-	134	124	-	4.1	3.1	-	474	499
Belgium									
- Flemish Community	-	129	110	-	3.9	2.8	-	502	499
- French Community*	90	120	117	2.9	3.6	2.9	447	467	415
Canada	-	119	122	-	3.6	3.1	-	468	472
(British Columbia)	109	-	-	3.5	-	-	468	-	-
Czech Republic	-	137	121	-	4.2	3.0	-	496	513
Denmark*	n.a.	118	118	n.a.	3.6	3.0	n.a.	443	423
Finland	88	-	-	2.8	-	-	517	-	-
France	91	107	107	2.9	3.2	2.7	500	484	446
Germany*[5]	-	124	139	-	3.8	3.5	-	448	463
- TFGDR	110	-	-	3.5	-	-	470	-	-
- FTFR	95	-	-	3.1	-	-	473	-	-
Greece*	87	124	118	2.8	3.8	3.0	467	422	439
Hungary	100	131	119	3.2	4.0	3.0	488	471	497
Iceland	107	105	113	3.5	3.2	2.8	485	435	442
Ireland	102	132	134	3.3	4.0	3.4	467	462	471
Italy	99	-	-	3.2	-	-	467	-	-
Japan	-	140	118	-	4.2	3.0	-	536	514
Korea	-	142	125	-	4.3	3.1	-	540	504
Netherlands*	94	127	114	3.0	3.8	2.9	472	477	505
New Zealand	136	127	136	4.4	3.8	3.4	485	443	458
Norway	90	115	118	2.9	3.5	3.0	473	445	470
Portugal	73	84	102	2.4	2.5	2.6	485	411	429
Spain	87	100	106	2.8	3.0	2.7	451	436	465
Sweden	107	119	122	3.5	3.6	3.1	493	460	476
Switzerland	98	122	127	3.2	3.7	3.2	494	485	460
United Kingdom									
- England	-	127	141	-	3.8	3.5	-	443	484
- Scotland*	-	123	133	-	3.7	3.3	-	436	451
United States	126	128	143	4.1	3.9	3.6	477	435	465
Average of above	*99*	*123*	*123*	*3.2*	*3.7*	*3.1*	*478*	*463*	*469*

- : The country did not participate in that part of the study. n.a. : not available.
* Countries did not satisfy one or more TIMSS sampling guidelines.
1. Population II, "14-year-olds", for reading; "8th grade" students with a majority of 13-year-olds for mathematics and science. "7th grade" students for Denmark.
2. The average difference registered between the reading scores of the 9-year-old and the 14-year-old samples tested is 155 points. The average progress in reading in a school year is estimated to be around 31 points. On this basis, one can consider that the gap between the 25th and the 75th percentile of 14-year-old students is the equivalent of approximately two years of schooling in Portugal, and around four years in New Zealand.
3. The average difference registered between the scores in mathematics of the 7th and 8th grade samples tested is 33 points. On this basis, one can consider that the gap observed in the 8th grade between the 25th and the 75th percentile of the students is the equivalent of approximatively four years of schooling in Korea, and two years and a half in Portugal.

Data for Figure 4.2 *(continued)*

	75th percentile (in points) for:			25th percentile minus international mean (in equivalent year's progress)			75th percentile minus international mean (in equivalent year's progress)		
	Reading	Mathematics	Science	Reading	Mathematics	Science	Reading	Mathematics	Science
Australia*	-	600	619	-	-2.1	-1.7	-	2.4	2.9
Austria*	-	608	623	-	-1.6	-1.0	-	2.7	3.0
Belgium									
- Flemish Community	-	631	609	-	-0.7	-1.0	-	3.4	2.6
- French Community*	537	587	532	-1.7	-1.9	-3.7	1.2	2.0	0.1
Canada	-	587	594	-	-1.8	-1.8	-	2.0	2.1
(British Columbia)	577	-	-	-1.0	-	-	2.5	-	-
Czech Republic	-	633	634	-	-0.9	-0.5	-	3.5	3.4
Denmark*	n.a.	561	541	n.a.	-2.6	-3.4	n.a.	1.2	0.4
Finland	605	-	-	0.5	-	-	3.4	-	-
France	591	591	553	0.0	-1.3	-2.7	2.9	2.1	0.8
Germany* [5]	-	572	602	-	-2.5	-2.1	-	1.5	2.4
- TFGDR	580	-	-	-1.0	-	-	2.6	-	-
- FTFR	569	-	-	-0.9	-	-	2.2	-	-
Greece*	554	546	557	-1.1	-3.3	-2.9	1.7	0.7	0.9
Hungary	588	602	616	-0.4	-1.7	-1.0	2.8	2.5	2.8
Iceland	592	540	555	-0.5	-2.9	-2.8	3.0	0.5	0.8
Ireland	569	594	605	-1.1	-2.0	-1.9	2.2	2.2	2.5
Italy	566	-	-	-1.1	-	-	2.1	-	-
Japan	-	676	632	-	0.4	-0.5	-	4.9	3.3
Korea	-	682	629	-	0.5	-0.8	-	5.1	3.2
Netherlands*	566	604	619	-0.9	-1.5	-0.8	2.1	2.5	2.9
New Zealand	621	570	594	-0.5	-2.6	-2.3	3.9	1.5	2.1
Norway	563	560	588	-0.9	-2.6	-1.9	2.0	1.1	1.9
Portugal	559	495	531	-0.5	-3.7	-3.2	1.9	-1.0	0.1
Spain	539	536	571	-1.6	-2.9	-2.1	1.3	0.4	1.4
Sweden	600	579	598	-0.2	-2.1	-1.7	3.2	1.7	2.2
Switzerland	592	607	587	-0.2	-1.3	-2.2	3.0	2.6	1.9
United Kingdom									
- England	-	570	625	-	-2.6	-1.5	-	1.5	3.1
- Scotland*	-	559	584	-	-2.9	-2.5	-	1.1	1.8
United States	603	563	608	-0.7	-2.9	-2.1	3.3	1.2	2.5
Average of above	577	586	592	-0.7	-2.0	-1.9	2.5	2.0	2.0

4. The average difference registered between the scores in science of the 7th and 8th grade samples tested is 40 points. On this basis, one can consider that the gap observed in the 8th grade between the 25th and the 75th percentile of the students is the equivalent of approximatively three years and a half of schooling in Australia and two years and a half in Portugal.

5. Germany TFGDR refers to the territory of the former Democratic Republic; FTFR refers to the former territory of the Federal Republic.

Sources: IEA, Reading Literacy Study; and IEA, Third International Mathematics and Science Study.

Data for Figure 4.3
Achievement scores of students older than the norm[1](difference from national mean, on index from -1 to +1)

	Percentage of "over-aged" students[1] in Reading Literacy sample	Reading handicap of the "over-aged" students[2]	Percentage of "over-aged" students[3] in TIMSS sample	Mathematics handicap of the "over-aged" students[2]	Science handicap of the "over-aged" students[2]
Australia*	-	-	13.8	-0.045	-0.043
Austria*	-	-	12.7	-0.582	-0.491
Belgium					
- Flemish Community	-	-	17.4	-0.858	-0.626
- French Community*	33.4	-0.713	24.0	-0.858	-0.618
Canada	-	-	13.1	-0.431	-0.514
(British Columbia)	10.6	-0.786	-	-	-
Czech Republic	-	-	8.9	-0.855	-0.645
Denmark*	n.a.	n.a.	7.3	-0.594	-0.406
Finland	1.2	(-1.100)	-	-	-
France	28.4	-0.730	24.2	-0.6223	-0.426
Germany* [4]	-	-	16.8	-0.487	-0.439
- TFGDR	4.1	(-0.904)	-	-	-
- FTFR	17.1	-0.634	-	-	-
Greece*	7.4	-0.735	10.4	-0.752	-0.565
Hungary	7.5	-0.994	10.5	-0.980	-0.749
Iceland	0.8	(-1.572)	0.6	(-1.104)	(-0.877)
Ireland	13.2	-0.563	12.7	-0.493	-0.322
Italy	16.1	-0.674	-	-	-
Japan	-	-	0.1	(-0.498)	(-0.810)
Korea	-	-	4.0	(-0.555)	(-0.408)
Netherlands*	17.6	-0.573	18.6	-0.607	-0.416
New Zealand	4.6	(-1.004)	8.2	-0.430	-0.370
Norway	3.5	(-0.743)	2.1	(-0.486)	(-0.711)
Portugal	34.1	-0.495	25.1	-0.544	-0.439
Spain	19.8	-0.717	20.3	-0.625	-0.378
Sweden	2.0	(-0.931)	3.3	(-0.872)	-0.685
Switzerland	19.3	-0.441	17.6	-0.519	-0.459
United Kingdom					
- England	-	-	1.0	(-0.261)	(-0.040)
- Scotland*	-	-	3.6	(-0.401)	(-0.417)
United States	17.4	-0.852	14.8	-0.569	-0.431
Average of above	*13.6*	*-0.725*	*11.8*	*-0.605*	*-0.475*

-: The country did not participate in that part of the study. n.a. : not available. * Countries did not satisfy one or more TIMSS sampling guidelines.
1. Students at least 8 months older than the average age in the grade concerned.
2. The "handicap" of "over-aged" students is the standardised difference between their average scores and the average scores of "normal aged" students. This estimate is not sufficiently reliable when the group of "over-aged" students is very small (less than 5 per cent). In such cases the results are given in parentheses.
3. Students at least 6 months older than the mean of the grade. The "over-aged" students could not be defined in the same way for both studies due to the difference in the design of the studies.
4. Germany TFGDR refers to the territory of the former Democratic Republic; FTFR refers to the former territory of the Federal Republic.
Sources: IEA, Reading Literacy Study; and IEA, Third International Mathematics and Science Study.

Data for Figure 4.4
Students not enrolled, 1995[1,2] (percentage of the relevant age group)

	Final legal compulsory schooling age	Typical graduation age, upper secondary	Not enrolled at:		
			Final legal compulsory schooling	Age 17	At typical graduation age, upper secondary
Australia	15	19	1.9	6.5	47.2
Austria	17	17-19	12.3	12.3	38.3
Belgium[3]	18	18-20	12.5	-0.1	22.9
Canada	16	18	6.0	20.9	38.1
Czech Republic	15	18-19	1.3	28.3	66.0
Denmark	16	19-22	6.2	18.3	54.4
Finland	16	19	7.4	9.5	58.5
France	16	18-20	3.9	7.4	30.2
Germany[3]	18	19	15.7	6.4	34.6
Greece	14.5	18-19	11.4	44.2	53.6
Hungary	16	17-18	11.8	28.9	41.3
Ireland	15	17-18	4.4	19.1	22.9
Japan[4]	15	18	-1.2	5.6	-
Korea	14	18	1.4	10.4	45.9
Luxembourg[5]	15	18-19	20.1	22.3	-
Mexico	15	18	48.0	63.0	75.3
Netherlands[3]	18	18-19	17.5	6.7	23.7
New Zealand	16	18	0.1	23.2	43.4
Norway	16	19	5.0	9.7	50.8
Portugal	14	18	10.7	27.2	44.6
Spain	16	16-18	17.3	25.2	27.2
Sweden	16	19	3.0	4.2	64.7
Switzerland	15	18-20	2.5	16.5	44.6
Turkey	14	17	44.3	74.3	74.3
United Kingdom	16	16-18	13.1	25.3	29.8
United States	17	18	21.4	21.4	44.4
Average of above	*15-16*	*18-19*	*11.5*	*20.6*	*44.9*

-: missing value.
1. Data refer to full- and part-time enrolments in all levels and types of education, attending both public and private institutions.
2. Net enrolment rates for 17-year-olds.
3. Full-time compulsory schooling lasts until age 15 or 16; after that schooling is compulsory on a part-time basis until age 18.
4. Enrolment at age 17 is underestimated. Data for tertiary levels are missing.
5. Net enrolment rates by single year of age are underestimated since they only include those students who attend a public or publicly funded school in Luxembourg. Students who are residents of Luxembourg but attend either a not publicly funded school in Luxembourg or a school in a neighbouring country are excluded.
Source: OECD Education Database.

Data for Figure 4.5
Percentage of all 16-35 year-olds in the labour force at low and high literacy levels by labour force status,[1] and earnings,[2] 1994

		Document scale			
		Levels 1 and 2 combined		Levels 3 and 4/5 combined	
Canada	Unemployed	14.1	(2.9)	6.9	(2.4)
	Employed with low or no income	36.0	(3.4)	27.7	(2.7)
	Employed with medium to high income	37.7	(6.1)	50.0	(4.9)
	Employed (no income information)	12.1	(4.2)	15.4	(3.1)
Ireland	Unemployed	25.8	(4.1)	11.7	(2.2)
	Employed with low or no income	34.9	(3.1)	27.6	(3.8)
	Employed with medium to high income	31.7	(2.1)	52.0	(3.2)
	Employed (no income information)	7.7*	(1.7)	8.7	(1.7)
Netherlands	Unemployed	16.2*	(2.8)	5.6	(1.0)
	Employed with low or no income	28.7	(3.8)	36.0	(1.9)
	Employed with medium to high income	43.5	(3.0)	52.8	(1.8)
	Employed (no income information)	11.5*	(2.0)	5.6	(0.9)
United Kingdom	Unemployed	23.7	(2.3)	8.8	(1.5)
	Employed with low or no income	38.1	(2.9)	31.5	(2.4)
	Employed with medium to high income	36.2	(2.5)	57.8	(2.5)
	Employed (no income information)	2.0*	(0.6)	1.9*	(0.6)
United States	Unemployed	9.0	(1.8)	4.9*	(1.6)
	Employed with low or no income	57.1	(3.2)	49.5	(4.0)
	Employed with medium to high income	16.1	(2.0)	35.0	(3.0)
	Employed (no income information)	17.7	(2.6)	10.6	(2.2)
Average of above	*Unemployed*	*17.8*		*7.6*	
	Employed with low or no income	*39.0*		*34.5*	
	Employed with medium to high income	*33.0*		*49.5*	
	Employed (no income information)	*10.2*		*8.4*	

Standard errors of estimates in brackets.
1. Population excludes those who are students and those not in the labour force.
2. Earnings are deemed "low" for those in the bottom two quintiles of earners, and "medium" to "high" for those in the top three quintiles.
* Sample size is insufficient to obtain a reliable estimate.

Source: OECD and Statistics Canada, International Adult Literacy Survey.

Chapter 5

Data for Figure 5.1
**Percentage of three age groups enrolled in tertiary-level education,
public and private, 1985, 1990 and 1995[1,2]**

	Ages 18-21			Ages 22-25			Ages 26-29		
	1985	1990	1995	1985	1990	1995	1985	1990	1995
Belgium	24.5	-	40.7	7.2	-	16.5	1.5	-	3.6
Canada	25.5	28.9	37.9	9.5	11.4	21.7	3.0	3.4	9.2
Denmark	7.4	7.4	8.9	16.3	17.9	22.6	8.2	9.3	11.2
Finland	9.3	13.6	17.5	17.3	20.7	27.4	7.9	10.2	12.9
France	19.4	24.6	34.2	10.0	11.8	17.7	4.3	3.9	4.6
Germany	8.8	8.5▌	10.6	15.5	15.9▌	17.0	8.9	10.4▌	11.4
Ireland*	15.2	20.3	27.2	2.8	4.3	15.5	-	-	-
Netherlands	14.4	17.9	23.2	11.9	13.4	18.7	5.7	4.7	5.6
New Zealand	14.9	20.8	28.6	9.6	13.8	13.3	-	-	7.2
Norway	8.8	14.4	17.5	13.2	18.9	23.6	5.7	8.2	10.0
Portugal	5.8	-	17.9	5.4	-	15.7	2.3	-	5.9
Spain	14.9	21.2	25.6	10.6	13.5	17.5	4.0	4.5	5.5
Sweden	7.9	8.7	13.0	11.3	11.4	16.6	6.5	6.1	7.5
Switzerland	5.7	6.4	7.7	10.6	12.1	14.7	5.2	6.4	7.2
Turkey	-	7.4	10.1	-	4.6	7.4	-	2.3	3.4
United Kingdom	-	16.1	25.8	-	4.7	9.3	-	-	4.8
United States	33.0	36.2	34.7	14.5	17.1	20.7	8.2	8.5	10.5
Average of above	*14.4*	*16.8*	*22.4*	*11.0*	*12.8*	*17.4*	*5.5*	*6.5*	*7.5*

-: missing value.
* Data for 22-25 age group include ages 26-29.
1. Net enrolment rates based on head counts.
2. Vertical bars indicate a break in the series.
Source: OECD Education Database.

Data for Figure 5.2a
**Ratio of upper secondary graduates to population at typical age of graduation (times 100),
by type of programme and gender, 1995[1]**

	Total			General			Vocational and apprenticeship		
	M + W	Men	Women	M + W	Men	Women	M + W	Men	Women
Australia	-	-	-	64.9	59.1	70.9	-	-	-
Belgium (Flemish Community)	110.1	95.2	117.1	33.4	29.1	37.9	76.4	70.4	82.4
Canada	71.7	68.1	75.4	71.7	68.1	75.4	-	-	-
Czech Republic	78.0	78.8	77.1	10.3	7.8	13.0	67.6	71.0	64.2
Denmark	81.3	75.9	86.8	45.7	37.7	54.0	35.6	38.2	32.8
Finland	102.3	94.9	110.1	47.0	38.9	55.4	54.7	55.5	53.9
France	87.3	85.5	89.2	38.0	32.3	43.9	49.3	53.2	45.3
Germany	88.0	88.5	87.4	24.4	21.7	27.2	63.6	66.8	60.2
Greece	79.5	75.2	84.1	51.1	43.4	59.2	28.4	31.8	24.9
Hungary	76.5	85.8	88.2	16.6	17.4	26.8	57.7	66.0	58.8
Ireland*	93.8	87.1	100.8	88.9	82.5	95.6	4.9	4.6	5.2
Italy	67.0	63.8	70.4	17.7	15.3	20.3	48.2	47.6	48.8
Japan	94.1	90.9	97.6	69.1	65.6	72.9	25.0	25.3	24.7
Korea	85.4	85.7	85.1	50.3	54.2	46.2	35.1	31.5	38.9
Mexico	25.7	-	-	22.1	-	-	3.6	-	-
Netherlands	80.0	-	-	32.3	-	-	46.0	-	-
New Zealand	95.0	86.9	103.5	65.2	60.8	69.9	29.7	26.1	33.6
Norway	106.0	123.3	88.0	44.3	38.4	50.4	61.7	84.9	37.6
Spain	72.9	64.7	81.4	45.7	40.0	51.7	26.2	23.9	28.7
Sweden	63.8	59.9	68.0	25.5	17.5	33.8	37.7	41.9	33.2
Switzerland	79.4	84.1	74.6	18.5	16.2	20.9	60.9	67.9	53.7
Turkey	37.1	42.6	31.4	21.9	23.9	19.8	15.5	19.1	11.8
United States	75.8	70.5	81.3	75.8	70.5	81.3	-	-	-
Average of above	*79.6*	*80.4*	*84.9*	*42.6*	*40.0*	*48.9*	*41.4*	*45.9*	*41.0*

-: missing value, or data included in another category.
* "General" upper secondary education contains a number of strong vocational elements (Leaving Certificate Vocational Programme; Leaving Certificate Applied Programme).
1. First educational programmes only.
Source: OECD Education Database.

Data for Figure 5.2b
**Qualifications on entry into tertiary education in selected countries,
percentage distributions, various years**

Australia (1991, cross-section)

Commencing bachelor's (pass)	100
Complete final year of secondary education	55
Some tertiary education	26
Mature age/employment experience entry	6
Other assessment/admission methods	13

Denmark (1993, modeled cohort analysis)

All participants	100
General upper secondary	75
Vocational upper secondary	15
Other	10

France (1995-96, cross-section)

First-year entrants	100
New baccalauréat – general	62
New baccalauréat – technological	23
New baccalauréat – vocational	2
Other*	13

Japan (1995, cross-section)

First-year entrants of high-school graduates	100
General secondary	85
Vocational secondary	15

United Kingdom (provisional 1994/95, cross-section)

First-degree and diploma students	100
A-levels	65
Vocational qualifications (NVQ, GNVQ)	8
Other (access, conversion courses; professional qualifications)	27

* Category "other" includes students with a baccalauréat examination who changed programmes as well as students with some tertiary experience.

Sources: Department of Employment, Education and Training, *National Report on Australia's Higher Education Sector*, 1993; Ministry of Education (Denmark), *Thematic Review of Tertiary Education*, January 1996; Ministère de l'Éducation nationale, de l'Enseignement supérieur et de la Recherche (France), Projections à un et deux ans des principales filières de l'enseignement supérieur, *Note d'Information, 97.21*, April, 1997; K. Yoshimoto, "*VOTEC and School-to-Work Transition in Japan*", National Institute of Multimedia Education, November, 1995; Department for Education and Employment (United Kingdom), *Thematic Review of Tertiary Education Policies*, 1996.

Data for Figure 5.3a
Women as a percentage of new entrants to the first stage of tertiary education, 1995

	Non-university tertiary education	University education
Austria	69.0	52.0
Canada	45.9	57.0
Czech Republic	65.7	-
Denmark	36.6	60.1
Finland	63.8	50.8
Germany	58.6	45.4
Hungary	-	51.0
Ireland*	49.7	49.7
Italy	62.0	52.0
Korea	49.9	44.2
Netherlands	-	52.0
New Zealand	51.1	57.3
Norway	58.2	58.3
Portugal	57.2	58.9
Spain	49.2	54.1
Sweden	-	55.8
Switzerland	32.9	45.3
Turkey	42.7	35.5
United Kingdom	54.3	49.8
United States	58.6	55.8
Average of above	*53.3*	*51.8*

-: missing value, or data included in another category.
* Full-time students only.
Source: OECD Education Database.

Data for Figure 5.3b
Percentage of new entrants into tertiary education who are women, selected subjects, 1995

	Total: all fields of study	Fine and applied arts, humanities, religion and theology, and documentation	Social and behavioural sciences, commercial and business administration, law, mass communication	Natural science, mathematics and computer science	Medical science and health-related studies	Trade, craft, and industrial engineering, architecture and town planning, transport and communications	Education science and teacher training, agriculture, forestry and fishery, home economics (domestic science), service trades, and other programmes
Non-university							
Austria	69.0	85.0	69.0	18.2	87.9	32.0	75.4
Canada	45.9	43.8	65.1	33.0	71.1	15.2	54.6
Czech Republic	64.6	45.9	62.3	0.0	84.2	34.3	82.2
Denmark	36.6	79.3	32.2	0.0	83.1	15.0	49.1
Finland	63.8	63.2	80.8	19.3	89.1	9.9	68.6
Germany	58.6	65.1	48.4	27.8	75.7	9.0	75.1
Japan	67.4	76.5	60.1	89.2	76.1	15.7	93.4
Norway	58.2	65.8	50.1	48.3	88.8	19.7	64.2
New Zealand	51.1	58.8	54.5	53.0	83.7	16.6	67.3
Portugal	57.2	59.0	60.4	36.9	82.5	26.8	76.6
Switzerland	32.9	64.7	34.0	37.1	78.3	5.0	60.9
Turkey	42.7	49.9	45.7	19.2	71.8	15.8	51.5
Average of non-university	*54.0*	*63.1*	*55.2*	*31.8*	*81.0*	*17.9*	*68.2*
University							
Austria	52.0	68.7	53.2	34.3	61.9	21.0	69.4
Canada	57.0	61.6	56.2	43.9	80.1	20.5	62.0
Denmark	60.1	69.5	39.5	21.0	91.9	17.3	68.7
Finland	50.8	74.9	58.6	36.4	86.9	15.3	69.5
Germany	45.4	67.0	46.5	32.8	54.3	18.5	62.3
Iceland	56.8	63.1	49.5	41.1	75.8	6.9	74.1
Italy	52.1	76.3	52.9	48.4	57.9	20.4	71.4
Japan	34.4	67.2	22.6	26.1	54.2	8.3	54.7
Netherlands	52.0	55.5	51.6	25.6	79.9	10.5	63.3
Norway	58.4	64.0	45.5	40.3	86.0	13.8	67.5
New Zealand	57.3	65.8	54.9	41.8	72.8	28.1	67.3
Portugal	58.9	73.3	60.5	52.0	68.0	31.5	70.4
Spain	54.1	64.5	56.6	41.8	75.0	26.1	72.2
Sweden	55.8	67.8	57.8	36.3	83.7	18.9	73.3
Switzerland	45.3	60.0	45.9	29.7	56.9	18.4	68.2
Turkey	35.5	49.1	31.8	43.1	52.1	25.2	38.6
Average of university	*51.6*	*65.5*	*49.0*	*37.2*	*71.1*	*18.8*	*65.8*

Values for men can be obtained by substracting shown data values from the 100 per cent total.
Source: OECD Education Database.

Data for Figure 5.4
Percentage distribution of first-time new entrants into public and private tertiary education institutions, first stage, by age group, 1995

	Non-university				University			
	Ages 25 and under	Ages 26-34	Ages 35 and over	All ages (numbers)	Ages 25 and under	Ages 26-34	Ages 35 and over	All ages (numbers)
Austria	-	-	-	7 186	89.2	8.0	2.8	27 822
Canada	60.4	19.4	18.1	208 063	79.2	10.4	9.0	202 786
Denmark	58.9	31.1	9.9	10 772	72.0	19.1	8.9	23 812
France	100.0	-	-	139 444	100.0	-	-	253 609
Germany	-	-	-	128 372	83.8	13.2	2.6	266 736
Greece	98.1	1.9	-	20 469	95.4	4.6	-	24 696
Hungary	-	-	-	-	71.1	15.3	-	65 550
Ireland	98.9	1.1	-	14 123	97.7	2.0	-	17 477
Netherlands	-	-	-	-	87.9	6.6	5.5	69 890
New Zealand	50.5	22.0	27.4	10 842	76.9	11.6	11.5	21 509
Norway	82.1	9.7	8.3	16 892	68.7	15.8	15.5	15 947
Sweden	-	-	-	-	72.4	16.1	11.5	62 381
Switzerland	50.9	49.1	-	29 580	89.3	10.7	-	13 619
Turkey	78.6	14.2	7.2	109 848	89.8	8.5	1.6	194 540
United Kingdom	52.0	23.7	24.3	246 113	77.5	12.4	10.1	320 168
United States	62.9	37.1	-	2 005 351	83.0	17.0	-	1 867 019
Average of above	*72.1*	*20.9*	*15.9*	*226 697*	*83.4*	*11.4*	*7.9*	*215 473*

-: missing or negligible value, or data included in another category.
Hungary: University-level education, first stage includes advanced degrees.
Ireland: Full-time students only.
Sweden: University-level education, first stage includes non-university tertiary education.
Greece, Hungary, Ireland, Switzerland and United States: Ages 26-34 category includes students aged 35 and over.
Source: OECD Education Database.

Data for Figure 5.5
Percentage of non-university tertiary education in total tertiary enrolment, first stage, 1995

	Total tertiary enrolment, first stage (numbers)	Share of non-university tertiary in total enrolment, first stage (percentages)
Australia	840 873	45.9
Austria	212 669	9.0
Belgium	332 540	55.8
Canada	1 667 112	46.9
Czech Republic	171 740	16.4
Denmark	102 172	17.1
Finland	188 272	22.7
Germany	2 155 728	13.1
Greece	296 357	30.6
Hungary	87 626	-
Iceland*	7 251	17.5
Ireland	112 249	45.4
Italy	1 755 018	5.4
Japan	3 778 957	33.6
Korea	2 111 256	27.2
Mexico	1 354 426	10.1
Netherlands	284 744	-
New Zealand	143 814	33.0
Norway	126 956	40.1
Portugal	286 852	22.4
Spain	1 470 381	1.6
Sweden	230 437	-
Switzerland	133 884	46.2
Turkey	1 107 320	26.8
United Kingdom	1 507 041	32.6
United States	12 262 613	45.1
Average of above	*1 258 780*	*28.0*

-: missing or negligible value, or data included in another category.
* Full-time students only.
Source: OECD Education Database.

Data for Figure 5.6
Initial destinations in tertiary education by entry qualifications, selected countries (per cent of students)

France (1995, cross section)

Entering tertiary education	
Baccalauréat – General	100
University	72
Preparatory classes for *grandes écoles* (CPGE)	13
University institutes of technology (IUT)	8
Advanced technician sections of *lycées* (STS)	7
Baccalauréat – Technological	100
University	30
Preparatory classes for *grandes écoles* (CPGE)	1
University institutes of technology (IUT)	13
Advanced technician sections of *lycées* (STS)	56

Germany (1992, cross-section)

Entering tertiary education (FTFR)	
Higher education entrance qualifications	100
University	79
Fachhochschule	21
Fachhochschule entrance qualifications	100
University	8
Fachhochschule	92
Entering tertiary education (new *Länder*, 1993)	100
Higher education entrance qualifications	75
University	25
Fachhochschule	
Fachhochschule entrance qualifications	100
University	1
Fachhochschule	99

Japan (1995, cross-section)

Entering tertiary education	
General high-school graduate	100
University	45
Junior college or special training school	55
Vocational high-school graduate	100
University	21
Junior college or special training school	79

Source: OECD Secretariat.

Data for Figure 5.7
Non-completion rates in tertiary education in selected countries, various years[1] (percentages)

	Fail in first year	Fail to complete programme	Fail to complete any programme
Belgium (Flemish Community), 1994			
University	47	34	
Non-university (one-cycle)	50	39	
Belgium (French Community), 1992-94			
University	56-62	57	
Non-university	60	38	
Denmark, 1995			
Tertiary		40	23
France, 1993[2]			
Total tertiary, excl. Sections de Techniciens Supérieurs		27	
University Institutes of Technology		20	
Italy, late 1980s			
Tertiary			64
Germany, 1993-94			
Tertiary			29-31
United Kingdom, 1995			
Tertiary			6-13

1. Figures have been drawn from several sources, and are therefore subject to differences in coverage and methodology. For definitions and methodology, readers are referred to the sources mentioned. Further work to improve the comparative information base is needed.
2. The figures refer to those who changed programmes or dropped out after the first year; first-cycle only.

Sources: Belgium (French Community), Germany, Italy, United Kingdom: Jean-Louis Moortgat (1996), *A Study of Dropout in European Higher Education*, Council of Europe; Belgium (Flemish Community): J.C.Verhoeven and I. Beuselinck (1996), *Higher Education in Flanders (Belgium): A Report for the OECD*, Ministry of the Flemish Community; Denmark: Ministry of Education (1997), Communication to the Secretariat; France: Ministère de l'Éducation nationale, de l'Enseignement supérieur et de la Recherche, *Les entrants et les accédants : principales caractéristiques —Poursuites dans la filière et réorientations après 7 ans des entrants de 1993* (tabled data supplied for OECD "Thematic Review of the First Years of Tertiary Education").

ALSO AVAILABLE

Literacy, Economy and Society
Results of the First International Adult Literacy Survey
(OECD and Statistics Canada) (1995)
ISBN 92-64-14655-5
FF210   £26   US$40   DM60

Lifelong Learning for All (1996)
ISBN 92-64-14815-9
FF255   £33   US$50   DM74

Education at a Glance – OECD Indicators (1996)
ISBN 92-64-15356-X
FF 260   £34   US$50   DM76

Education at a Glance – Analysis (1996)
ISBN 92-64-15357-8
FF 50   £6   US$10   DM15

Literacy Skills for the Knowledge Society (1997)
Further Results of the First International Adult Literacy Survey
ISBN 92-64-15624-0
FF 180   £23   US$35   DM53

Education at a Glance – OECD Indicators (1997)
ISBN 92-64-15622-4
FF 260   £27   US$43   DM77

MAIN SALES OUTLETS OF OECD PUBLICATIONS
PRINCIPAUX POINTS DE VENTE DES PUBLICATIONS DE L'OCDE

AUSTRALIA – AUSTRALIE
D.A. Information Services
648 Whitehorse Road, P.O.B 163
Mitcham, Victoria 3132   Tel. (03) 9210.7777
                              Fax: (03) 9210.7788

AUSTRIA – AUTRICHE
Gerold & Co.
Graben 31
Wien I   Tel. (0222) 533.50.14
                              Fax: (0222) 512.47.31.29

BELGIUM – BELGIQUE
Jean De Lannoy
Avenue du Roi, Koningslaan 202
B-1060 Bruxelles   Tel. (02) 538.51.69/538.08.41
                              Fax: (02) 538.08.41

CANADA
Renouf Publishing Company Ltd.
5369 Canotek Road
Unit 1
Ottawa, Ont. K1J 9J3   Tel. (613) 745.2665
                              Fax: (613) 745.7660

Stores:
71 1/2 Sparks Street
Ottawa, Ont. K1P 5R1   Tel. (613) 238.8985
                              Fax: (613) 238.6041

12 Adelaide Street West
Toronto, QN M5H 1L6   Tel. (416) 363.3171
                              Fax: (416) 363.5963

Les Éditions La Liberté Inc.
3020 Chemin Sainte-Foy
Sainte-Foy, PQ G1X 3V6   Tel. (418) 658.3763
                              Fax: (418) 658.3763

Federal Publications Inc.
165 University Avenue, Suite 701
Toronto, ON M5H 3B8   Tel. (416) 860.1611
                              Fax: (416) 860.1608

Les Publications Fédérales
1185 Université
Montréal, QC H3B 3A7   Tel. (514) 954.1633
                              Fax: (514) 954.1635

CHINA – CHINE
Book Dept., China National Publications
Import and Export Corporation (CNPIEC)
16 Gongti E. Road, Chaoyang District
Beijing 100020   Tel. (10) 6506-6688 Ext. 8402
                              (10) 6506-3101

CHINESE TAIPEI – TAIPEI CHINOIS
Good Faith Worldwide Int'l. Co. Ltd.
9th Floor, No. 118, Sec. 2
Chung Hsiao E. Road
Taipei   Tel. (02) 391.7396/391.7397
                              Fax: (02) 394.9176

**CZECH REPUBLIC –
RÉPUBLIQUE TCHÈQUE**
National Information Centre
NIS – prodejna
Konviktská 5
Praha 1 – 113 57   Tel. (02) 24.23.09.07
                              Fax: (02) 24.22.94.33
E-mail: nkposp@dec.niz.cz
Internet: http://www.nis.cz

DENMARK – DANEMARK
Munksgaard Book and Subscription Service
35, Nørre Søgade, P.O. Box 2148
DK-1016 København K   Tel. (33) 12.85.70
                              Fax: (33) 12.93.87

J. H. Schultz Information A/S,
Herstedvang 12,
DK – 2620 Albertslung   Tel. 43 63 23 00
                              Fax: 43 63 19 69

Internet: s-info@inet.uni-c.dk

EGYPT – ÉGYPTE
The Middle East Observer
41 Sherif Street
Cairo   Tel. (2) 392.6919
                              Fax: (2) 360.6804

FINLAND – FINLANDE
Akateeminen Kirjakauppa
Keskuskatu 1, P.O. Box 128
00100 Helsinki

Subscription Services/Agence d'abonnements :
P.O. Box 23
00100 Helsinki   Tel. (358) 9.121.4403
                              Fax: (358) 9.121.4450

*FRANCE
OECD/OCDE
Mail Orders/Commandes par correspondance :
2, rue André-Pascal
75775 Paris Cedex 16   Tel. 33 (0)1.45.24.82.00
                        Fax: 33 (0)1.49.10.42.76
                        Telex: 640048 OCDE
Internet: Compte.PUBSINQ@oecd.org

Orders via Minitel, France only/
Commandes par Minitel, France exclusivement :
36 15 OCDE

OECD Bookshop/Librairie de l'OCDE :
33, rue Octave-Feuillet
75016 Paris   Tel. 33 (0)1.45.24.81.81
                        33 (0)1.45.24.81.67

Dawson
B.P. 40
91121 Palaiseau Cedex   Tel. 01.89.10.47.00
                              Fax: 01.64.54.83.26

Documentation Française
29, quai Voltaire
75007 Paris   Tel. 01.40.15.70.00

Economica
49, rue Héricart
75015 Paris   Tel. 01.45.78.12.92
                              Fax: 01.45.75.05.67

Gibert Jeune (Droit-Économie)
6, place Saint-Michel
75006 Paris   Tel. 01.43.25.91.19

Librairie du Commerce International
10, avenue d'Iéna
75016 Paris   Tel. 01.40.73.34.60

Librairie Dunod
Université Paris-Dauphine
Place du Maréchal-de-Lattre-de-Tassigny
75016 Paris   Tel. 01.44.05.40.13

Librairie Lavoisier
11, rue Lavoisier
75008 Paris   Tel. 01.42.65.39.95

Librairie des Sciences Politiques
30, rue Saint-Guillaume
75007 Paris   Tel. 01.45.48.36.02

P.U.F.
49, boulevard Saint-Michel
75005 Paris   Tel. 01.43.25.83.40

Librairie de l'Université
12a, rue Nazareth
13100 Aix-en-Provence   Tel. 04.42.26.18.08

Documentation Française
165, rue Garibaldi
69003 Lyon   Tel. 04.78.63.32.23

Librairie Decitre
29, place Bellecour
69002 Lyon   Tel. 04.72.40.54.54

Librairie Sauramps
Le Triangle
34967 Montpellier Cedex 2   Tel. 04.67.58.85.15
                              Fax: 04.67.58.27.36

A la Sorbonne Actual
23, rue de l'Hôtel-des-Postes
06000 Nice   Tel. 04.93.13.77.75
                              Fax: 04.93.80.75.69

GERMANY – ALLEMAGNE
OECD Bonn Centre
August-Bebel-Allee 6
D-53175 Bonn   Tel. (0228) 959.120
                        Fax: (0228) 959.12.17

GREECE – GRÈCE
Librairie Kauffmann
Stadiou 28
10564 Athens   Tel. (01) 32.55.321
                              Fax: (01) 32.30.320

HONG-KONG
Swindon Book Co. Ltd.
Astoria Bldg. 3F
34 Ashley Road, Tsimshatsui
Kowloon, Hong Kong   Tel. 2376.2062
                              Fax: 2376.0685

HUNGARY – HONGRIE
Euro Info Service
Margitsziget, Európa Ház
1138 Budapest   Tel. (1) 111.60.61
                              Fax: (1) 302.50.35
E-mail: euroinfo@mail.matav.hu
Internet: http://www.euroinfo.hu/index.html

ICELAND – ISLANDE
Mál og Menning
Laugavegi 18, Pósthólf 392
121 Reykjavik   Tel. (1) 552.4240
                              Fax: (1) 562.3523

INDIA – INDE
Oxford Book and Stationery Co.
Scindia House
New Delhi 110001   Tel. (11) 331.5896/5308
                         Fax: (11) 332.2639
E-mail: oxford.publ@axcess.net.in

17 Park Street
Calcutta 700016   Tel. 240832

INDONESIA – INDONÉSIE
Pdii-Lipi
P.O. Box 4298
Jakarta 12042   Tel. (21) 573.34.67
                              Fax: (21) 573.34.67

IRELAND – IRLANDE
Government Supplies Agency
Publications Section
4/5 Harcourt Road
Dublin 2   Tel. 661.31.11
                              Fax: 475.27.60

ISRAEL – ISRAËL
Praedicta
5 Shatner Street
P.O. Box 34030
Jerusalem 91430   Tel. (2) 652.84.90/1/2
                              Fax: (2) 652.84.93

R.O.Y. International
P.O. Box 13056
Tel Aviv 61130   Tel. (3) 546 1423
                              Fax: (3) 546 1442
E-mail: royil@netvision.net.il

Palestinian Authority/Middle East:
INDEX Information Services
P.O.B. 19502
Jerusalem   Tel. (2) 627.16.34
                              Fax: (2) 627.12.19

ITALY – ITALIE
Libreria Commissionaria Sansoni
Via Duca di Calabria, 1/1
50125 Firenze   Tel. (055) 64.54.15
                              Fax: (055) 64.12.57
E-mail: licosa@ftbcc.it

Via Bartolini 29
20155 Milano   Tel. (02) 36.50.83

Editrice e Libreria Herder
Piazza Montecitorio 120
00186 Roma   Tel. 679.46.28
                              Fax: 678.47.51

Libreria Hoepli
Via Hoepli 5
20121 Milano   Tel. (02) 86.54.46
                              Fax: (02) 805.28.86

Libreria Scientifica
Dott. Lucio de Biasio 'Aeiou'
Via Coronelli, 6
20146 Milano   Tel. (02) 48.95.45.52
                                Fax: (02) 48.95.45.48

JAPAN – JAPON
OECD Tokyo Centre
Landic Akasaka Building
2-3-4 Akasaka, Minato-ku
Tokyo 107   Tel. (81.3) 3586.2016
                                Fax: (81.3) 3584.7929

KOREA – CORÉE
Kyobo Book Centre Co. Ltd.
P.O. Box 1658, Kwang Hwa Moon
Seoul   Tel. 730.78.91
                                Fax: 735.00.30

MALAYSIA – MALAISIE
University of Malaya Bookshop
University of Malaya
P.O. Box 1127, Jalan Pantai Baru
59700 Kuala Lumpur
Malaysia   Tel. 756.5000/756.5425
                                Fax: 756.3246

MEXICO – MEXIQUE
OECD Mexico Centre
Edificio INFOTEC
Av. San Fernando no. 37
Col. Toriello Guerra
Tlalpan C.P. 14050
Mexico D.F.   Tel. (525) 528.10.38
                                Fax: (525) 606.13.07
E-mail: ocde@rtn.net.mx

NETHERLANDS – PAYS-BAS
SDU Uitgeverij Plantijnstraat
Externe Fondsen
Postbus 20014
2500 EA's-Gravenhage   Tel. (070) 37.89.880
Voor bestellingen: Fax: (070) 34.75.778

Subscription Agency/   Agence d'abonnements :
SWETS & ZEITLINGER BV
Heereweg 347B
P.O. Box 830
2160 SZ Lisse   Tel. 252.435.111
                                Fax: 252.415.888

**NEW ZEALAND –
NOUVELLE-ZÉLANDE**
GPLegislation Services
P.O. Box 12418
Thorndon, Wellington   Tel. (04) 496.5655
                                Fax: (04) 496.5698

NORWAY – NORVÈGE
NIC INFO A/S
Ostensjoveien 18
P.O. Box 6512 Etterstad
0606 Oslo   Tel. (22) 97.45.00
                                Fax: (22) 97.45.45

PAKISTAN
Mirza Book Agency
65 Shahrah Quaid-E-Azam
Lahore 54000   Tel. (42) 735.36.01
                                Fax: (42) 576.37.14

PHILIPPINE – PHILIPPINES
International Booksource Center Inc.
Rm 179/920 Cityland 10 Condo Tower 2
HV dela Costa Ext cor Valero St.
Makati Metro Manila   Tel. (632) 817 9676
                                Fax: (632) 817 1741

POLAND – POLOGNE
Ars Polona
00-950 Warszawa
Krakowskie Prezdmiescie 7   Tel. (22) 264760
                                Fax: (22) 265334

PORTUGAL
Livraria Portugal
Rua do Carmo 70-74
Apart. 2681
1200 Lisboa   Tel. (01) 347.49.82/5
                                Fax: (01) 347.02.64

SINGAPORE – SINGAPOUR
Ashgate Publishing
Asia Pacific Pte. Ltd
Golden Wheel Building, 04-03
41, Kallang Pudding Road
Singapore 349316   Tel. 741.5166
                                Fax: 742.9356

SPAIN – ESPAGNE
Mundi-Prensa Libros S.A.
Castelló 37, Apartado 1223
Madrid 28001   Tel. (91) 431.33.99
                                Fax: (91) 575.39.98
E-mail: mundiprensa@tsai.es
Internet: http://www.mundiprensa.es

Mundi-Prensa Barcelona
Consell de Cent No. 391
08009 – Barcelona   Tel. (93) 488.34.92
                                Fax: (93) 487.76.59

Libreria de la Generalitat
Palau Moja
Rambla dels Estudis, 118
08002 – Barcelona
               (Suscripciones) Tel. (93) 318.80.12
               (Publicaciones) Tel. (93) 302.67.23
                                Fax: (93) 412.18.54

SRI LANKA
Centre for Policy Research
c/o Colombo Agencies Ltd.
No. 300-304, Galle Road
Colombo 3   Tel. (1) 574240, 573551-2
                                Fax: (1) 575394, 510711

SWEDEN – SUÈDE
CE Fritzes AB
S–106 47 Stockholm   Tel. (08) 690.90.90
                                Fax: (08) 20.50.21

For electronic publications only/
Publications électroniques seulement
STATISTICS SWEDEN
Informationsservice
S-115 81 Stockholm   Tel. 8 783 5066
                                Fax: 8 783 4045

Subscription Agency/Agence d'abonnements :
Wennergren-Williams Info AB
P.O. Box 1305
171 25 Solna   Tel. (08) 705.97.50
                                Fax: (08) 27.00.71

Liber distribution
Internatinal organizations
Fagerstagatan 21
S-163 52 Spanga

SWITZERLAND – SUISSE
Maditec S.A. (Books and Periodicals/Livres
et périodiques)
Chemin des Palettes 4
Case postale 266
1020 Renens VD 1   Tel. (021) 635.08.65
                                Fax: (021) 635.07.80

Librairie Payot S.A.
4, place Pépinet
CP 3212
1002 Lausanne   Tel. (021) 320.25.11
                                Fax: (021) 320.25.14

Librairie Unilivres
6, rue de Candolle
1205 Genève   Tel. (022) 320.26.23
                                Fax: (022) 329.73.18

Subscription Agency/Agence d'abonnements :
Dynapresse Marketing S.A.
38, avenue Vibert
1227 Carouge   Tel. (022) 308.08.70
                                Fax: (022) 308.07.99

See also – Voir aussi :
OECD Bonn Centre
August-Bebel-Allee 6
D-53175 Bonn (Germany)   Tel. (0228) 959.120
                                Fax: (0228) 959.12.17

THAILAND – THAÏLANDE
Suksit Siam Co. Ltd.
113, 115 Fuang Nakhon Rd.
Opp. Wat Rajbopith
Bangkok 10200   Tel. (662) 225.9531/2
                                Fax: (662) 222.5188

**TRINIDAD & TOBAGO, CARIBBEAN
TRINITÉ-ET-TOBAGO, CARAÏBES**
Systematics Studies Limited
9 Watts Street
Curepe
Trinidad & Tobago, W.I.   Tel. (1809) 645.3475
                                Fax: (1809) 662.5654
E-mail: tobe@trinidad.net

TUNISIA – TUNISIE
Grande Librairie Spécialisée
Fendri Ali
Avenue Haffouz Imm El-Intilaka
Bloc B 1 Sfax 3000   Tel. (216-4) 296 855
                                Fax: (216-4) 298.270

TURKEY – TURQUIE
Kültür Yayinlari Is-Türk Ltd.
Atatürk Bulvari No. 191/Kat 13
06684 Kavaklidere/Ankara
                                Tel. (312) 428.11.40 Ext. 2458
                                Fax : (312) 417.24.90
Dolmabahce Cad. No. 29
Besiktas/Istanbul   Tel. (212) 260 7188

UNITED KINGDOM – ROYAUME-UNI
The Stationery Office Ltd.
Postal orders only:
P.O. Box 276, London SW8 5DT
Gen. enquiries   Tel. (171) 873 0011
                                Fax: (171) 873 8463

The Stationery Office Ltd.
Postal orders only:
49 High Holborn, London WC1V 6HB
Branches at: Belfast, Birmingham, Bristol,
Edinburgh, Manchester

UNITED STATES – ÉTATS-UNIS
OECD Washington Center
2001 L Street N.W., Suite 650
Washington, D.C. 20036-4922 Tel. (202) 785.6323
                                Fax: (202) 785.0350
Internet: washcont@oecd.org

Subscriptions to OECD periodicals may also be
placed through main subscription agencies.

Les abonnements aux publications périodiques de
l'OCDE peuvent être souscrits auprès des
principales agences d'abonnement.

Orders and inquiries from countries where Distribu-
tors have not yet been appointed should be sent to:
OECD Publications, 2, rue André-Pascal, 75775
Paris Cedex 16, France.

Les commandes provenant de pays où l'OCDE n'a
pas encore désigné de distributeur peuvent être
adressées aux Éditions de l'OCDE, 2, rue André-
Pascal, 75775 Paris Cedex 16, France.

                                        12-1996

OECD PUBLICATIONS, 2, rue André-Pascal, 75775 PARIS CEDEX 16
PRINTED IN FRANCE
(96 97 05 1) ISBN 92-64-15682-8 – No. 49639 1997